Age Discrimination

Sue Thompson

TiP Theory into Practice

Series Editor Neil Thompson

RHP

Russell House Publishing

First published in 2005 by:
Russell House Publishing Ltd.
4 St. George's House
Uplyme Road
Lyme Regis
Dorset DT7 3LS
Tel: 01297-443948
Fax: 01297-442722
e-mail: help@russellhouse.co.uk
www.russellhouse.co.uk

British Library Cataloguing-in-publication Data:

A catalogue record for this book is available from the British Library.

ISBN: 1-903855-59-4

Typeset by TW Typesetting, Plymouth, Devon
Printed by Alden, Oxford

About Russell House Publishing

RHP is a group of social work, probation, education and youth and community work practitioners and academics working in collaboration with a professional publishing team.

Our aim is to work closely with the field to produce innovative and valuable materials to help managers, trainers, practitioners and students.

We are keen to receive feedback on publications and new ideas for future projects.

For details of our other publications please visit our website or ask us for a catalogue. Contact details are on this page.

Contents

The Theory into Practice Series

This exciting new series fills a significant gap in the market for short, user-friendly texts, written by experts, that succinctly introduce sets of theoretical ideas, relate them clearly to practice issues, and guide the reader to further learning. They particularly address discrimination, oppression, equality and diversity. They can be read either as general overviews of particular areas of theory and practice, or as foundations for further study. The series will be invaluable across the human services, including social work and social care; youth and community work; criminal and community justice work; counselling; advice work; housing; and aspects of health care.

About the Series Editor

Neil Thompson is a Director of Avenue Consulting Ltd (www.avenueconsulting.co.uk), a company offering training and consultancy in relation to social work and human relations issues. He was formerly Professor of Applied Social Studies at Staffordshire University. He has over 100 publications to his name, including best-selling textbooks, papers in scholarly journals and training and open learning materials.

Neil is a Fellow of the Chartered Institute of Personnel and Development, the Institute of Training and Occupational Learning and the Royal Society of Arts (elected on the basis of his contribution to organisational learning). He is the editor of the *British Journal of Occupational Learning* (www.traininginstitute.co.uk). He was also responsible for the setting up of the self-help website, www.humansolutions.org.uk. His personal website is at www.neilthompson.info.

Prospective authors wishing to make a contribution to the *Theory into Practice* series should contact Neil via his company website, www.avenueconsulting.co.uk.

Series Editor's Foreword

About the series

The relationship between theory and practice is one that has puzzled practitioners and theorists alike for some considerable time, and there still remains considerable debate about how the two interconnect. However, what is clear is that it is dangerous to tackle the complex problems encountered in 'people work' without having at least a basic understanding of what makes people tick, of how the social context plays a part in both the problems we address and the solutions we seek. Working with people and their problems is difficult and demanding work. To try to undertake it without being armed with a sound professional knowledge base is a very risky strategy indeed, and potentially a disastrous one.

An approach to practice based mainly on guesswork, untested assumptions, habit and copying others is clearly not one that can be supported. Good practice must be an *informed* practice, with actions based, as far as possible, on reasoning, understanding and evidence. This series is intended to develop just such good practice by providing:

- an introductory overview of a particular area of theory or professional knowledge;
- an exploration of how it relates to practice issues;
- a consideration of how the theory base can help tackle discrimination and oppression; and
- a guide to further learning.

The texts in the series are written by people with extensive knowledge and practical experience in the fields concerned and are intended as an introduction to the wider and more in-depth literature base.

About this book

This particular text, with its focus on age discrimination, explores an important range of issues. While some forms of discrimination, such as racism and sexism, have received widespread and in-depth attention, issues of age discrimination continue to receive a relatively low profile. We clearly still have a long way to go in putting ageism and its associated problems firmly on the agenda. This book, then, can play a significant role in raising awareness of the extent, nature and significance of age discrimination. In this regard, it is an important book.

Ageism is a term that is normally associated with older people, but Sue Thompson ably shows how age discrimination can also apply to children and young people. Ageism refers to unfair discrimination on the grounds of age and so, in principle, can apply at any age in the life course. However, given the significance of cultural and structural factors in shaping the experience of discrimination, the extremes of that life course render children and young people at one pole, and older people at the other, particularly vulnerable to being disadvantaged.

This well-written, well-informed book provides an excellent foundation for developing a clear understanding of age discrimination, how it comes about, how it can be avoided and how it can be challenged.

Neil Thompson, Series Editor

About the author

Sue Thompson is a Director of Avenue Consulting Ltd (www.avenueconsulting.co.uk), a company offering training and consultancy in relation to such problems as discrimination, stress, conflict, bullying and harassment and loss, grief and trauma.

Sue has extensive experience in the caring professions as a nurse, care manager and social worker. She is the author of *From Where I'm Sitting*, a training manual on work with older people (Russell House Publishing, 2002), as well as a number of book chapters and articles. She has co-written (with Neil Thompson) *Understanding Social Care* (Russell House Publishing, 2002) and *Community Care* (Russell House Publishing, 2005). She was also involved in developing the self-help website, www.humansolutions.org.uk.

Acknowledgements

I would like to thank Geoffrey at Russell House for his patience, and Neil for his moral and practical support in this and, indeed, all of my endeavours.

Introduction

So why a book about age discrimination? The response to that question lies in an understanding of what constitutes ageism, how powerful a process it is and, most importantly, the seriousness of the consequences it has for those it affects. As we will see, ageism is a process that makes it seem acceptable or legitimate to discriminate on the grounds of one factor – a person's age. That is to say it allows us to think about whole groups of people purely in terms of their age, regardless of other factors such as ability, experience, social and cultural background or personality, and to treat them differently and often less favourably because of that perception.

In the light of topical discussions such as whether life-saving medical technology should be denied older adults, and whether people should be forced to retire on the assumption that younger workers are more productive, it would be easy to think of ageism as relating solely to the experiences of older people, the most commonly used definition being those aged 60 years and older. However, we should not forget those at the opposite end of the age spectrum. It is not unusual for children and adolescents to be discriminated against on the grounds of their age too, and to be treated less favourably than adults whose voices are more powerful and whose right to have those voices heard is accepted more readily. Throughout the course of the discussions that follow there will perhaps be more of a focus on ageism as it affects older people, as this reflects my own career background, but I would urge readers to also keep in mind those who are denied opportunity and respect because of their youth. The aim of this book is to raise awareness of ageism as a discriminatory process so that its power can be undermined, and while some topics may have particular relevance for those at one end of the spectrum or the other, most should have something to say to those working in the fields of childcare, youth and community work, children's rights and so on, as well as those working with older people in residential settings, hospitals, community-based projects, local authorities and public services.

An exploration of what constitutes ageism will also raise the question of how it operates and why it is as pervasive and powerful a force as it is. Why, for example, do such issues as the ridicule of older people, and age discrimination in the workplace fail to attract the same level of social disapproval that racist and sexist attitudes and behaviour do? Part of the answer lies in the way that this form of discrimination goes largely unnoticed. It has become 'part of the wallpaper' in that it tends to be accepted as the norm, even to the extent that those who are discriminated against are either unaware of the extent of that discrimination or do recognise it, but feel themselves undeserving of anything better (see the discussion of 'internalised oppression' in Part One).

This book has fairly modest aims. It is an introduction to the topic of age discrimination, although it is hoped that it will inspire you to go on to read other publications and engage in more complex debates. Age discrimination is too powerful a force, and its implications too diverse, for a simple anti-ageist panacea to be prescribed. If this book raises your awareness of where and how ageism is operating, so that it no longer passes unnoticed or unchallenged, then it will have succeeded in its aim. What you do with that awareness will be largely up to you. Ensuring that your own practice is underpinned by anti-ageist values is a major step in the right direction. If you can also raise awareness, and perhaps promote change, at the level of your organisation's culture and practices then you will be playing an even more vital part in the anti-ageist challenge. This book may well have modest aims but, as the saying goes, 'big trees from little acorns grow'.

As with other publications in this series, *Age Discrimination* is divided into four parts:

The theory base: Part One introduces a framework for analysing discrimination. This framework is used as an aid to understanding how oppression operates across the board, before moving on to examine how it can be applied to help us understand age discrimination in particular. It discusses how ageism operates at a number of levels, not only that of personal prejudice and ageist behaviour, but also at the level of our shared culture (media representations and so on) and within institutions such as the education and health systems.

The implications for practice: Part Two moves on to integrate theory with practice and help you to consider whether your practices either reinforce or challenge ageism. Of course, this is not to suggest that anti-ageist practice is purely a matter of individual responsibility and action – far from it. Applying the framework explored in Part One highlights the extent to which ageism needs to be understood and addressed at levels which go far beyond the individual.

Tackling discrimination and oppression: Ageism, by its very definition, is a form of oppression in itself. However, recognition has to be given to the fact that it does not operate in isolation from, or independently of, other forms of oppression, such as disablism, sexism, racism, heterosexism and so on. Part Three explores these interactions, highlighting and challenging the tendency to ignore or minimise other aspects of identity under a blanket description of 'old' or 'young'.

Guide to further learning: As mentioned earlier, this book is an introductory text. Covering every detail of this complex subject, or every aspect of its implications for practice, is beyond its scope. Part Four guides you to other reading material which will help you develop your understanding to a higher level, or focus on a particular area of practice – or indeed both. It also includes details of relevant websites that might complement or extend your learning.

Introduction

Getting to grips with what age discrimination is, and what it does, requires us to consider how society is structured around different aspects of our identity and background. We might think of ourselves as free-thinking individuals, and to a great extent we are, but we also have to recognise that other factors have a significant effect on how and where we live our lives and what life opportunities we have access to. It makes a difference, for example, whether we are rich or poor, whether we are from an ethnic majority or minority, whether we are male or female, disabled or able-bodied, and so on. As we will see from the discussions that follow, it also matters whether we are considered to be 'in our prime' or too young or old to be taken seriously or accorded respect. It makes a difference because of power. That is to say, some groups in society have more power than others to have their interests promoted. It is this unequal distribution of power that underpins discrimination and, in order to promote an understanding of the processes involved in discrimination on the grounds of age, this section first explores discrimination in general before going on to focus more specifically on ageism itself.

The remainder of Part One consists of four sections:

- an explanation of some of the key terms used in relation to ageism;
- a discussion about the different levels at which discrimination can be seen to operate;
- an exploration of the processes through which ageism manifests itself; and
- a consideration of the power of stereotypes and cultural expectations to oppress those at both ends of the life course.

Key terms

This book is an introduction to the subject, and it may well be the case that some of the concepts referred to are new to you, or that you are not absolutely sure of their meaning when used in contexts such as this. For that reason, this section begins with a brief overview of some of key terms used throughout the book.

Discrimination: This is the process, or more accurately set of processes, which has the effect of disadvantaging some individuals or groups. In its most literal form the word just means to differentiate or mark out as different. So, for example, one could use it to discriminate *between* two sets of students attending a lecture at their university, those using English as their first language and those using Urdu. If the lecture was delivered through the medium of English only it could be argued that the Urdu-speaking students were put at a disadvantage and thereby discriminated *against*. In the context of the discussions in this book it is this latter sense of the word that is being referred to – that which attaches connotations of disadvantage and not just difference.

Oppression: This is the end result of discrimination as defined above, in that it refers to an unfair use of power by one social group over another. As Thompson (2001) suggests, oppression is:

> Inhuman or degrading treatment of individuals or groups; hardship and injustice brought about by the dominance of one group over another; the negative and demeaning exercise of power. (p. 34)

This abuse of power is not necessarily intentional and often goes unnoticed and unchallenged because cultural practices become so familiar that we fail to notice what is happening around us, or that social institutions such as the family, the economy and the legal system are playing a part in perpetuating them. For example property rights have, until very recently, been based on traditional family values and social arrangements such as that of heterosexual marriage. It could be argued that this, in disadvantaging those who choose to live in gay or lesbian relationships, has been an abuse of power which has been oppressive on the grounds of sexual orientation. This is, of course, only one example but the key point to take on board is that oppression is the outcome of discrimination which, in turn, is based on the actual or perceived *experiencing* of unequal power relations.

Stereotyping: There is so much information available to us as we go about our daily lives that we have to find some way of making that information manageable. One way in which we do this is to attribute characteristics to a particular group, on the assumption that these characteristics typify that particular group. For example the mention of the concept 'teenager' tends to conjure up, in many people's minds, a sullen, argumentative and socially awkward young person. And yet we probably all know of teenagers who bear no resemblance to this 'typification'. Using such a framework, while helping to prevent 'information overload', can also lead to disadvantage if the typifications are allowed to become stereotypes. That is to say, if we refuse to alter our perceptions, even in the face of evidence that contradicts the typification (such as all those teenagers who are helpful, confident, well-adjusted and so on), then the typification becomes a stereotype. As Thompson (2003) suggests, the process of stereotyping is one that can lead to negative labels being attached when they do not represent the reality of a situation:

> A stereotype is a typification that is maintained despite evidence to the contrary – that is, we continue to treat the person concerned as if he or she were typical of a

particular category, when in fact this is not the case or, indeed, when the typification itself is inaccurate and based on derogatory assumptions. In short, typifications are helpful, stereotypes are not. (p. 31)

Ageism: This is a form of oppression which results from individuals being discriminated against purely on the grounds of age as an indicator of competence. The term is most often used to refer to the way in which people in the latter stages of their lives are treated less favourably than their younger counterparts but, as this book will demonstrate, children and young people can also be the victims of ageist attitudes and practices. As we shall see, this form of discrimination can occur at a number of levels and is not confined to that of personal prejudice.

Ethnicity: 'Ethnic' is a term which is often used misleadingly to refer to something, or someone, as 'exotic'. For example, we often hear it being used to refer to jewellery, fashion items, artwork, furniture or ideas that originate in a culture that is different from our own. That is, some people tend to see others as 'ethnic' but would not relate this to their own identity. However, given that ethnicity is about 'belongingness' to a community or group, it is something which is a feature of *everyone's* existence – we all have an ethnic identity. It is sometimes used interchangeably with the term 'race' but, as Blakemore and Boneham (1994) suggest, it can incorporate a much wider range of features, including a shared:

- history or homeland;
- language;
- religion; and/or
- culture, including issues such as dress, ritual, diet, social norms and so on.

Values: This is an extremely important concept which underpins any form of 'people work' but one that is difficult to put into words. As argued elsewhere by Thompson and Thompson, 'values are such an influence on everything we do and say, how we live our lives and how we carry out our work, that we do have to engage with the subject if our practice is to have a positive impact on the lives of those for whom we provide.' (Thompson and Thompson, 2002, p. 20). Values are, quite literally, those ideas that we value or hold dear and which affect what we do. For example, if you value the right to human dignity, then you would probably oppose torture and the maltreatment of vulnerable people. Similarly, if you value free speech then you would find it difficult to have your opinions stifled, or to see it happening to someone else. However, this is not just a personal issue. Whole sets of ideas are underpinned by shared assumptions about what is important. Consider the following, for example: family values, political values, religious values and so on.

Ideology: Here we have another concept that is difficult to put into words, but one which needs to be highlighted because of its close link with the issue of power. At a very basic level, ideologies are sets of ideas or ways of looking at the world and how it operates. For example, there are political ideologies which have their basis in particular sets of ideas about how power should be shared, feminist ideologies which espouse ideas about gender roles, and so on. The reason ideology is being discussed in the context of a book about ageism is because oppression often results from one group or faction in society becoming more powerful than another and benefiting from a disproportionate share of prestige, power and resources. That is, an ideology becomes a *dominant* ideology.

One way in which certain ideologies maintain their dominant status is by becoming 'invisible'. That is, we fail to notice that they are operating to keep things the way that the dominant group wants them to be and we become so accustomed to the status quo that we are unlikely to challenge it. In the discussions which follow you will see how this relates to ageism.

Partnership: This is quite a 'buzzword' at the moment and one which is used in a variety of ways. It denotes a way of working, and an underpinning value base, in which people work together towards mutually acceptable ends. Partnership is about sharing ideas, expertise and responsibilities and is a relationship that can exist in a number of contexts, such as that between different agencies, as explored by Harrison *et al*. (2003) or between service providers and service users (Beresford and Croft, 1993;Thornton and Tozer, 1995; Thompson 2002a). In terms of age discrimination, it is this latter interpretation which will be most relevant, because it serves to challenge the idea that older people and children have little to contribute to decision-making processes.

Social constructionism: This is an approach, or more accurately a set of approaches, which challenges the notion that social definitions and roles are fixed and 'natural' constants. As Burr (1995) comments:

> Social constructionism cautions us to be ever suspicious of our assumptions about how the world appears to be. This means that the categories with which we as human beings apprehend the world do not necessarily refer to real divisions. For example, just because we think of some music as 'classical' and some as 'pop' does not mean we should assume that there is anything in the nature of the music itself that means it has to be divided up in that particular way. (p. 3)

Social constructionism focuses on how we imbue concepts with meaning according to how we understand the world around us, and that these meanings are only specific to a particular cultural or historic context. For example, the concept of childhood has not always meant what it tends to mean now and expectations of what children and parents should do has changed over centuries. As Aries (1962) points out, the term itself is relatively new historically, as there was a time when there was no concept of children as being any different from adults. Similarly, the definition of old age is one that is open to interpretation. Ask yourself whether there is a specific point in life's journey when one suddenly switches, in a biological sense, from being young to being old. A social constructionist perspective would suggest that the definition has more to do with how we understand concepts in a way that is specific to how we live our lives. For example, in British society in the 21st century, retirement policy still tends to inform our definition of old age as being 60 years and over, but this may change over time as more and more people retire earlier, or we may move away from defining old age with reference to working practices.

Exercise 1.1

Think carefully about the following words. What thoughts or feelings do they bring out for you?

Child	Old
Teenager	Elderly
Adolescent	Pensioner

Does this raise any issues for you about how age is very significant in our society?

All of these key terms are complex and contested concepts, which is to say that there is no one 'truth' about these matters. They have long been debated and will no doubt continue to be topics of debate. As such, this brief overview cannot begin to do them justice, but as you work through this book you may come to appreciate how important they are in the context of a discussion about ageism and its effects. As the title suggests, this book is specifically about furthering our understanding of discrimination on the grounds of age, but before moving on to the specifics of ageism, it would be useful to first look at how discrimination can be theorised at a more general level.

Levels of discrimination

When the subject of discrimination is raised it is often talked about at the level of individual thoughts and actions. That is to say, it is conceptualised as a matter of personal prejudice. For example, *she* is racist, *he* is sexist, *I* don't discriminate, and so on. However, we only have to think about recent investigations highlighted in the media, such as alleged racism in police forces (Marlow and Loveday, 2000) and rationing of resources in health and social care provision (Henwood and Harding, 2002) to see that there is the potential for discrimination also to occur at the level of social institutions and structures. That is, the discriminatory attitudes and practices are embedded in the fabric of society and its institutions, and the way they operate. At this level we can see that whole areas of organisational policy making and working practice can be premised on discriminatory attitudes and, while it may not be intentional, the end result can still be that some groups are treated less favourably than others.

Thompson (2001) proposes a useful framework, what he refers to as PCS analysis, for helping us to understand that, in order to appreciate the harmful effects of discrimination and oppression, we need to move beyond explanations that focus on the level of personal attitudes and actions. He argues that discrimination can be seen to operate at three separate, but interconnected, levels:

- the personal;
- the cultural; and
- the structural.

Furthermore, these levels operate within a particular relationship, so that in order to understand individual attitudes and actions we need to consider the cultural context in which we live our lives and the influence that shared ideas about what is 'right and proper' have on us as individuals. However, if we were to leave it at that, we would fail to take on board that these shared ideas are not arrived at randomly but, as discussed below, are in turn influenced by the power of dominant individuals, groups and movements to have their ideas and interests promoted.

The personal level

As discussed earlier, discrimination can manifest itself at this level, most frequently in the form of personal prejudice. We all make judgements as a necessary part of our daily lives, but prejudice involves making negative judgements about people, usually on the basis of stereotypes, as we will see when we move on to look at the cultural level. Examples of discrimination at this level might be the man who demeans or belittles women, or the person who verbally or physically abuses gay people. Sometimes it is the case that such attitudes and behaviour have their roots in personal experience, which can then affect how that person sees matters from then on. For example, someone who is assaulted by someone with a particular accent or ethnic characteristic may associate that type of behaviour with that accent, skin colour or whatever, and develop a prejudicial attitude to all people with those characteristics.

In some cases the discriminatory attitudes are intentional and overt, such as where people proudly display their allegiance to racist organisations but, as we will discuss later, it is sometimes the case that individuals are not sufficiently self-aware to recognise that they are speaking or behaving in a way that displays prejudicial values or assumptions.

While it is the case that some individuals are indeed racist or sexist, or discriminate on the grounds of *their* personal views about people's worth, to see discrimination wholly in these terms is to miss the wider context in which society is structured and the way in which issues beyond the personal level affect our lives.

Of course it is true that we operate as individuals but it is also the case that we live out our individual lives within a cultural context and it is to this that we now turn.

The cultural level

Attitudes which might be expressed at a personal level are formed within the context of growing up within a particular culture at a particular time. As we grow up we form our own view of the world and begin to work out what is important to us. That is, we formulate a value base. At the same time we are being influenced by what is going on around us, being bombarded by messages from the media, our families, our teachers and so on. From these messages we pick up cues about what is, and is not, acceptable within our particular culture. For example, we learn that certain behaviours are appropriate to particular contexts, such as job interviews or funerals. We learn that there is a need to communicate at different levels and in different styles according to the context, so that we would probably not address a magistrate in a courtroom in the same way as we would chat to our friends on the telephone.

When we use 'culture' in this context we are not using the word in the sense that it is often used, that is to describe interests such as art appreciation and the opera, but to a more generalised concept – that of a shared set of meanings or 'unwritten rules'. One example of this would be practices around marriage. In some cultures there is a general consensus that marriage is a partnership between equals. In others it is accepted, and even celebrated, that a woman becomes the property of a husband on marriage. As we grow up within a culture we learn what its 'rules' are and, because they are so ingrained in the history of that culture, we hardly notice they are affecting how we think and act. In this way discrimination can operate unseen, as those with the power to do so can tailor what messages we receive to their interests, as we shall discuss when we move on to examine the structural level.

Exercise 1.2

What 'unwritten rules' about age are part of the culture you were brought up in? For example, what does your culture say about how older people fit into our society? And what does it say about children and young people?

Consider, for example, the 'rules' of sexuality in relation to:
  (a) child care;
  (b) older people.

What does your culture regard as acceptable or unacceptable in relation to those groups?

A particularly potent vehicle for discrimination at the cultural level is that of humour. Despite efforts to challenge them, jokes abound which denigrate and belittle certain groups of people. Consider how many jokes there are which promote long-entrenched ideas such as that all Irish people are stupid or that all gay men are effeminate. As we shall discuss later, older people are often the butt of humour which has its premise in negative assumptions about ageing.

We can see, then, that there is a relationship between the cultural level and the personal level, in that discrimination at a personal level is largely informed by attitudes and values which are promoted at the level of a shared culture. What we need to bear in mind as far as discrimination is concerned is that there is also a relationship between the cultural level and the structural level which deals with the bigger picture about how societies are organised and power relations maintained.

The structural level

If you have not come across the term 'structure' in fields of study such as sociology or social policy, it can be a difficult concept to get your head around in this context. A key point is that, while individuals behave independently and make decisions in their capacity as individuals, they do not do so without being influenced, and sometimes constrained, by the way that society is structured around them. In a more generalised context, 'structures' tend to suggest something fixed and concrete like a building. In the sense used here, structure refers to how societies are divided along lines such as class, race and gender and the term 'social institution' is used when referring to concepts such as the established church, the education system, the legal system, the economy and so on. Giddens (1997) offers several scenarios which help to explain the structural perspective. One of these is unemployment:

> When, in a city of 100,000, only one man is unemployed, that is his personal trouble, and for its relief we properly look to the character of the man, his skills and his immediate opportunities. But when, in a nation of 50 million employees, 15 million men are unemployed, that is an issue, and we may not hope to find its solution within the range of opportunities open to any one individual . . . Both the correct statement of the problem and the range of possible solutions require us to consider the economic and political institutions of the society, and not merely the personal situation and character of a scatter of individuals. (p. 11)

Giddens is making the point that an individualistic perspective can neglect to appreciate how wider factors can impinge on personal experience. For example, in the above scenario, it is suggested that when the percentage of unemployed people in a population is so high, it is necessary to look beyond individual fecklessness as a cause and consider whether issues such as high interest rates on loans, or detrimental trade agreements, might account for high unemployment more satisfactorily. Similarly, there are those who seek to explain high levels of youth crime in terms of aggressive or anti-social behaviour by 'bad' individuals, but a structuralist perspective would be more inclined to look at the significance of issues such as racism and poverty and the effect that they can have on people's life chances.

Exploring discrimination at this level helps us to understand why it is that negative stereotypes continue to be promoted as acceptable or are only selectively challenged. Cultural norms and expectations do not appear out of nowhere or operate within a vacuum. Just as the personal level is embedded within and informed by the cultural level, the latter needs to be appreciated in another context. As Thompson (2001) comments:

> But even this cultural context needs to be understood in terms of a wider context – the structural. That is, the C level is embedded within the S level. It is no coincidence that we have the cultural and social formations that currently exist. These owe much to the structure of society – the interlocking matrix of social divisions and the power relations which maintain them. (p. 23)

So, at this level, we can see that society is structured or divided on a number of bases including gender, class, race, ethnicity, sexual orientation, religion, and age. These are commonly referred to as 'social divisions'. As referred to earlier, prestige and resources are distributed according to these divisions and so this is not just abstract theorising for its own sake – these divisions *do* matter. If we are to understand how discrimination, and especially age discrimination, works and can be challenged then this level of analysis cannot be ignored.

For example, if educational curricula focus exclusively on the history of the United Kingdom from a white perspective then this approach gives out a message that the identities and contributions of other ethnic groups are of a lesser value, thereby helping to legitimate the right of the white majority to 'call the tune'. Similarly, a system of taxation which assumes that married women rely on their partners for their income serves to promote the message that this is how things should be, with the male partner earning money and the female partner rearing children. It is only fairly recently in UK society that these systems have begun to be altered to reflect women's changing role in the workforce, and the changes that have occurred in family structure. We might ask why this has been the case. Has it been, or indeed does it continue to be, in someone's or some group's interests to convince the population that the traditional nuclear family structure is what family *should* mean? This is too big a question to address here but, it might serve to get you thinking more about the role that structural issues play in discriminatory processes.

Practice Focus 1.1

Tomorrow was going to be a big day for Rita. Her family and friends had been busy for weeks arranging a party for her 85th birthday and she knew she was in for a hectic but enjoyable day. While making sure that her party clothes were in order, she noticed the collection of letters and keepsakes that she had kept at the bottom of her wardrobe and, although she had planned on having an early night, she couldn't resist taking a look. Amongst the papers she found the list she had made, as a young woman, on the night she had become engaged. She remembered that she had worried about how marriage might change her life and so had made a list of the places she wanted to visit and the things she wanted to do. Her intention had been to revisit this list from time to time, but she realised that she had never done so until now. As she unfolded the frail piece of paper she realised that she had not met a single one of those items on her 'wish list'. She had never been abroad. She had not gone back to working on the land, something she had enjoyed so much during the war years but had left once the war was over and she had a house and family to look after. And, despite being told by everyone that she had a wonderful acting talent, she had never made it into the world of drama that she had so aspired to.

At first Rita felt a sense of personal failure at how she had allowed herself to drift so far away from her ideals and plans. But as she lay on her bed, reminiscing to herself, she came to realise that it had not been as simple as that. Her husband had not earned a great deal but she had respected his wishes, and the customs of the day, by staying at home to raise their children. They had not gone hungry and never got into debt, but her travel plans had always been way beyond their means, especially when redundancy and industrial injury kept their income low. She would have been more than happy to contribute financially but had always been turned down in favour of men when applying for the manual jobs she knew she had been capable of. Later on in life, she had thought about travelling on her own but felt it wouldn't have been appropriate 'at her age' and, anyway, who would have looked after her husband? Carers for someone with Alzheimer's Disease were hard to find and she hadn't wanted to move him away from his familiar surroundings. And when she thought about her dreams of Hollywood fame, she began to smile to herself. It had been so unlikely to happen, especially for black women like herself.

Taking a last look at the list before returning it to its box, she thought about how naïve she had been as a young woman, not to realise the constraints she would face on her life's journey. Earlier in her life she had been influenced by dominant ideas around her gender and ethnicity but, as she had grown older, she realised that she had also let ageist stereotyping limit her horizons.

As we can see, the structures referred to here have the potential to be hugely influential. It should not be too difficult to see that those interest groups with the power to do so will make good use of them to get their values disseminated to a wide audience.

And so, having used PCS analysis to help us to understand the relationship between the different levels of discrimination, we will now move on to apply it more specifically to discrimination on the grounds of age. It will help us to highlight:

- the ways in which ageism operates;
- the significance of commonly held views about ageing; and
- the reasons why it continues to be a significant form of discrimination .

Furthering our understanding of the theoretical underpinnings of age discrimination should help us to plan a strategy for challenging it, something we will begin to address in Part Two.

And so let us now move on to look at ageism in particular.

Ageism

The personal level

As already noted, this is the level at which the attitudes and actions of individual people are grounded in personal prejudice. That is to say, it is the action or attitudes of individuals who discriminate on the grounds of age. One example would be a child who has waited his or her turn in a queue being ignored by a shop assistant, on the basis that adults are deemed to be more important. Another instance would be the person who shows a lack of respect to an older person by referring to him or her in a demeaning or degrading term such as 'fogey', or 'old codger'.

While comments and labels such as these can be very hurtful, it is important to bear in mind that discrimination at this level does not necessarily have to be intentional, although the fact remains that the outcome will still be discriminatory regardless of the intention. For example, it is not uncommon to come across individuals providing services for older people in need of care who refer to them as 'the geriatrics' or 'my old dears'. This suggests an underlying perception of exactly that: a group of service users, defined by their age and infirmity, rather than by their individual personalities. Some working in this field might object strongly to being accused of having prejudicial attitudes towards the very people they aim to support. This is not an issue of apportioning blame, but of highlighting that discrimination at the individual or personal level need not be overt or intentional, but it still operates to convey the message that it is acceptable to patronise some people on the grounds that they are less worthy of respect than others.

Practice Focus 1.2

Stanley was 72 years old and normally fit and healthy except for the occasional twinge of pain in his back and knees. He put this down to the many hours he spent digging and planting vegetables and flowers in his large garden and told his friends that it was worth a bit of pain for the pleasure, and meals, that his hobby provided him with. One Spring he slipped on some mud while mending a fence and, when the time came round for preparing the soil for the new seeds, he found himself laid up with a sprained ankle. Relatives and friends were all busy, and tried to persuade him to downsize his garden so that it took less time and effort to manage, now that he was 'getting on'. As he would hear nothing of this suggestion, one of his sons arranged for a couple of local residents to do the digging and planting for him. Stanley was pleased and felt very relieved that this offer of help would prevent him from getting too far behind in his gardening schedule. However, his delight soon turned to despair when the couple arrived and started to do the work. They put aside the detailed instructions he had written out and started to rearrange seed frames, flower beds and garden furniture to their own design. When he struggled out of his chair and limped across to show his alarm at what was happening to his garden he was met with a response that surprised and alarmed him even more. One called him 'grandad' and told him to go inside for a 'nice nap' while they got on with the work. The other told him they were going to put a concrete patio in, as requested by his son, so that he could have a container garden which would be easier for him to manage.

Seeing the garden he had designed and tended over the past forty years start disappearing before his eyes, he thanked them for their efforts but insisted that they both leave immediately.

At first, Stanley's son was unable to see why he had been so 'ungrateful', as he saw it but, on listening to things from his father's perspective, he began to see that he had been unintentionally ageist by taking away his father's rights to choice and autonomy. What had really brought this home to him was when Stanley had asked whether he would have arranged for his 38 year old sister's garden to have been revamped in this way, and without her permission, had she sprained her ankle.

This is also a feature of how people are treated at the other end of the age spectrum, although this is perhaps beginning to be addressed by recent moves to highlight children's rights. Despite progress in this field it remains the case that children and young people are often not treated with respect or enabled to have their opinions properly heard or acted on in contexts where their future care or life chances are being debated or decided (Inman, 2003; Thomas, 2001). As Director of Communications at The National Youth Agency, Spiers (2003) makes the point that politicians could use their influence to champion the interests of young people in their localities, as a way of challenging their misrepresentation in the mass media.

This tendency for both older and younger adults to be treated without respect for their opinions can perhaps be explained in terms of citizenship rights, or rather the denial of them. That is to say, children and young people are not seen as having earned the same rights as adults until they have reached the age of supposed maturity. Where older people are concerned it could be argued that, by withdrawing or being forced out of the world of work, they are no longer seen as being active contributors to society and so are deemed no longer worthy of citizenship rights and the respect that accompanies them. This is a complex debate and we will return to the concept of citizenship later. It is flagged up here as something to think about in terms of helping to explain why some individuals hold the views that they do.

The implications of such attitudes for practice with both older people and children are developed more fully in Part Two but, before moving on to consider how ageism can be seen to operate at the cultural level, it is worth giving a little more thought to why it is that some people feel the way that they do about older and younger people and give vent to those feelings in the ways described. As we will go on to discuss in more detail in Part Three, ageism is subtly different from other forms of discrimination in that it is something we are all, to some extent at least, likely to experience, 'from the inside'. That is to say, most of us will be able to recollect how it felt to experience our early years and, unless we die prematurely, we will all experience old age. And so, when we are thinking about old age, we are thinking about our future selves. For many people this is not something they wish to engage with. As we will explore in more detail later on, this could be something which contributes to a tendency to either:

- ignore these thoughts in the hope they will go away; or
- use ridicule or negativity to distance ourselves from that which we fear.

Exercise 1.3

Can you think of three ways in which your life might be better by the time you reach old age? Can you think of three ways in which it might be worse? Does this tell you anything about society's attitudes towards old age?

For other forms of discrimination we may not have that insider perspective. If we are white we will not have direct experience of what it is like to live in the world as a black person and to experience racism. If we are able-bodied we are unlikely to know what it feels like to experience disadvantage because of disablism, unless we become disabled as the result of accident or illness. Men will not know how it feels to experience life from a woman's perspective and vice versa. However, most of us will have the experience of being an older person in a society which values youth and vitality rather than age and experience and we may worry about what might face us as we grow older. Perhaps treating older people differently and with less respect is a way of saying 'I'm not like you' and a mechanism for dealing with one's own fears and insecurities about time marching on?

So far, we have concentrated on ageism at the personal level but, as we noted earlier, we live in a cultural context and it is to this that we now turn.

The cultural level

While ageism as expressed by individual attitudes and actions can be a discriminatory force in itself, we can see that it can become an even more potent form of oppression if these attitudes and actions are seen as legitimate by a whole culture. For example, if there is a cultural norm or accepted 'truth' which stipulates that children have a right to protection, then those who love and nurture their children will be applauded, while those who harm them will be vilified as child abusers. However, if it were seen as acceptable to treat children as if they were disposable (consider a time when sending very young children to work long hours in dangerous factories or in toxic atmospheres was seen as perfectly acceptable, as indeed it still is in some cultures), then those who treated them badly would not be thought badly of themselves.

If we consider the situation of older people we can see that there are rules and expectations about what is seen as acceptable in terms of aspiration and role. It must be recognised that there will be exceptions to the rule and that these views will not be shared by every single person but, in general, the cultural expectations about old age are that older people should not expect to do the following:

- remain in the workforce, although exceptions here would include those of high class or prestige (judges and so on) or in times of war or economic crisis;
- behave frivolously from time to time; or
- have sexual feelings or express a need for intimacy (Gibson, 1992; Bevan and Thompson, 2003).

At the other end of the age spectrum there are also rules about the status and expected behaviour of children and young people. Typically they should not expect to:

- be consulted about decisions that affect their lives;
- have much weight attached to their opinions because they are deemed to be inexperienced and naïve; or
- have their need to grieve recognised in situations where they experience a loss, including those of divorce or being received into care.

Such attitudes, while not shared by everyone are, nevertheless, very persuasive and influential ones. We see and hear these messages in a variety of media as we go about our daily lives. For example, have you ever tried to buy a birthday card for an older person which does not make a barbed reference to physical or mental decline, even if it is done in a supposedly humorous way? The fact that such cards sell in vast quantities suggests that the majority of people consider it acceptable to link old age with decrepitude in this way, even though the stereotype is often inaccurate. The term 'elderly' means simply 'old' but it implies 'decrepit', just as 'senile' also means simply 'old' but implies 'confused'. In cultures where older people are venerated the market for such cards would probably not exist because they would no doubt be considered to be offensive rather than funny.

Similarly, Midwinter (1990) comments on the way that old age is portrayed in television programmes. More often than not older people are portrayed in a negative manner, as objects of humour or ridicule. It would seem to be a case of 'damned if you are and damned if you are not' in that the characters are objects of humour either *because* they conform to expectations (consider Uncle Albert constantly reminiscing about the war in 'Only Fools and Horses' or Albert Steptoe being crotchety and set in his ways in 'Steptoe and Son') or because they throw the stereotype into relief (the athletic 'Supergran', or the nursing home resident who refused to live her days out quietly and graciously in 'Waiting for God'). Humour is an extremely powerful and efficient vehicle for transmitting ideas and the value we attach to them. It would seem that racist and sexist jokes are beginning to become less and less socially acceptable, and have even become recognised in law as offensive and degrading. The fact that ageist jokes and visual representations that portray older people as objects of ridicule do not appear to attract social disapproval would seem to support the assertion that ageism operates at a cultural as well as an individual level and that the latter operates within the context of the former.

Similarly, the fact that such important matters as children's rights (Baldwin, 2000) and their experience of grief across a whole range of loss situations (Kroll, 2002b; Romaine, 2002) have only recently been put on the agenda for research and action is an indication of how ideas operating at the cultural level help to downplay or even invisibilise the needs of this sector of the population. In cultural contexts where children and young people are highly valued then their needs are likely to be viewed more holistically. If the prevailing assumption is that children and youths are not 'real people' then their specific needs are less likely to be given a high profile.

So we can see that ageism works at a cultural level to legitimise the view that those at both ends of the age spectrum are 'less than' those who have already reached the designated age of majority but not yet reached the point at which society deems them to be peripheral to its needs. However, if we consider that societies and the cultural expectations which operate within them evolve rather than remain static, how can we explain why ageism continues to operate relatively unchallenged? Why is it that the shared understanding of old age is one of negativity, vulnerability and decline, even in the face of evidence to suggest that this is only partially true and often wildly inaccurate. Much of this can be addressed by looking at how ageism operates at the level of social structures and it is to this that we now turn.

The structural level

We have seen that discrimination on the grounds of age can arise out of personal prejudice but that those individual thoughts and actions arise out of a context in which the message 'children and older people do not matter that much – belittling or ignoring them and devaluing their contributions to society is no big deal' is one that is heard loud and often in the cultures in which we live and work. As we have already seen, the structural level is the level of vested interest. It helps provide an answer to the question 'why is it that such discriminatory messages fail to attract outrage?' because it points out to us that it is in the interests of important and influential organisations, systems and establishments that those at the outer edges of the age continuum are kept there.

One example of how ageism operates at the structural level is the matter of employment. At times of high unemployment employers have a wide pool of workers from which to draw, and it is likely that they will want to employ those whom they perceive to be 'best value for money'. If the prevailing cultural messages are that young people are feckless and untrustworthy and that older people have a tendency to be slow and stubborn, then employers will look to what they consider to be the 'prime' sector, hence the type of advertisements which stipulate that candidates must be over 25 or under 50. This then prevents many capable and competent workers who contradict the stereotypes from applying and, for as long as it suits those managing the economy to maintain those discriminatory practices, they are likely to go unchecked.

However, you may have noticed of late that older people in particular have had a much higher profile in particular work sectors, including shops and other service industries. Considering matters from a structural perspective, you might want to ask yourself whether practices that limit the age range from which employers can draw are now *not* in their interests, and that measures to outlaw age discrimination are beginning to attract approval for that very reason? Of course this is not to suggest that this is the only reason. The economy is a vastly complex institution and there are many competing perspectives on how and why it operates as it does. Nevertheless, this example should serve to highlight how age discrimination can operate at a level beyond both the individual and cultural levels.

Furthermore, if we consider the issue of compulsory retirement practices we can again see how structural matters contribute to a situation where relative poverty is a significant feature of old age, and particularly so for women (Vincent, 2003). From one perspective, this could be seen as a matter of individual failure to plan for the future, but can it be the case that all of those who are poor in old age find themselves so because they have not taken personal responsibility for providing for a time in their lives when their income would reduce? Analysts such as Walker (1993) would no doubt argue otherwise. His concept of 'structured dependency' is something we will return to in more detail in Part Three but, in essence, he suggests that these high levels of poverty in old age are largely a consequence of retirement policies (that is to say *political* policy) which are in turn underpinned by ideologies such as capitalism (*economic* policy) rather than of individual failing.

In this section we have looked briefly at the different levels at which ageism can be seen to operate. Before moving on to explore ageist processes, we need to remind ourselves that the three levels:

- individual action (often referred to as 'human agency');
- shared cultural 'rules'; and
- social stratification,

are all important in shaping experiences of discrimination.

Processes

The emphasis this far has been on the levels at which ageism can be seen to be operating. In this section we will move on to consider the ways in which it operates, that is to say the processes through which ageism manifests itself to the detriment of particular groups. Some of the discussions that follow will appear to be more relevant to the situation of older than younger people but, of course, age discrimination is not just about old age. Part Two will focus more particularly on the implications for practice but, as you read through this section, you might consider whether there are processes that you can identify with in the work undertaken with children and young people also. The list below is not intended to be comprehensive but should serve to highlight some of the more obvious ways in which ageism can be seen to operate. As we have already discussed, discrimination can operate in ways that are not immediately obvious and so it is to be hoped that, after reading this introductory text, you will be alert to its more subtle forms while carrying out the particular work that you do.

Welfarisation

This is the process whereby old age itself is conceptualised and promoted as a 'problem to be dealt with' by society. It is premised on the assumption that old age is necessarily a time of dependency even though statistical evidence suggests otherwise (DoH, 2001). It is testament to the power of stereotypes that the proportion of older people as a percentage of the general population has been portrayed in recent decades as a 'rising tide' waiting to swallow up vast amounts from the national purse. There has been much political debate about how the 'crisis' of care, caused by rising numbers of very old people (usually classed as those over 85 years), and falling numbers of those middle-aged relatives who most typically have provided support to them in the past, can be managed and afforded. It cannot be denied that there is an increasing risk of chronic illness and disability associated with ageing (Walker and Maltby, 1997). However this is not to say that *all* older people will become reliant on others. Indeed, figures from the General Household Survey in 2001, suggest that only 5 per cent of people over 65 consider that they are unable to provide themselves with a meal and only 14 per cent describe themselves as being unable to walk about outside without assistance. The survey claims that 4 per cent have the assistance of local authority helpers and 10 per cent the services of a private home help. While these figures need to be taken in the context of their being self-reported, which might not produce a totally accurate picture because of differences of interpretation and subjective experience, nevertheless they do suggest quite strongly that old age and dependency do not necessarily go together.

It is often enough to just hear or read in the media about the elderly population being described as a burden to fall into the trap of equating old age with dependency on welfare resources. However, those who work in the fields of health or social care may well get an even more biased view. When all of the people you work with day in and day out *do* need welfare provision it can become difficult to conceptualise older people in any other way and to think of old age only in negative terms. Rather than the specific medical or social issues that give rise to need being perceived as 'the problem' it is old age itself which is seen as needing to be addressed and, as a consequence, the link in people's minds between old age and decline is strengthened. Fennell *et al.* made the following comment in 1988 but it is still very apt:

> to approach the study of old age in terms only of problems and needs involves what Johnson (1976) has rightly termed a pathology model. We are prevented from seeing the whole picture and focusing it correctly, we see elderly people only in terms of their diseases, disabilities and deprivations. We focus unerringly on poverty, bereavement, social isolation, loneliness, role loss, illness, handicap, apathy and abuse. (pp. 6–7)

That the popular conception of old age continues to be one based on dependency, regardless of evidence to suggest that it is often a period of personal growth and productivity, highlights the power of ageist ideology to affect how we think and act.

Infantilisation

At its most basic, infantilisation is the process of treating an adult as if a child. There is certainly a case for treating children differently from adults since, physically and emotionally, they are usually less mature. It becomes a demeaning process when applied to older people because it assumes that they are different from other adults and less worthy of respect (Hockey and James, 1993; Thompson, 1995). It can be seen to be operating in situations such as those when older people are referred to by their first names only, without their permission, or by names such as 'pet' or 'dearie'. The use of such terms is not usually intended to be demeaning and may reflect a very tender and caring attitude on the part of those people who use them. Sometimes it just reflects a local tendency to call everyone by a common term such as 'luv', 'hen' or 'mate'. The issue is not that such terms should be dispensed with altogether but rather that the assumption that older people will not mind being referred to in such ways needs to be challenged.

Our names are a significant part of our identities and it is sometimes the case that we prefer different versions at different times and in different contexts. For example, I may be happy for a long-standing friend or a relative to refer to me by a pet name but would be offended should that term be used by a relative stranger from whom I would expect more respect. It comes down to a matter of choice and I would expect to be the one to make that choice. Denying me that right would seem to me to be disrespectful. Denying older people that right gives out the message 'your feelings don't matter. I respect you little enough to take the time to ask you how you would like to be addressed'.

Regardless of intention, the outcome of using pet names or first names without permission can be one of making an older person feel that they are being treated like a child. In a parent-child relationship it is usually the case that parents or carers make decisions on behalf of the child on the grounds that the former feel better equipped to make judgements on behalf of the latter. When an older person is treated in this way it reinforces the image of old age as one of dependency. And so, while the widespread use of pet names and forenames may seem to be fairly innocuous, it can have the devastating effect of making people feel disempowered. As noted earlier, ageism is the unfair treatment of people on the grounds of their age. Treating people like children, when they have already lived many decades as adults, must surely fall into that framework.

Practice Focus 1.3

Mrs Leung had been feeling physically unwell for several months after having an operation and her enforced convalescence was beginning to have an effect on her mental state too. She often felt tired and unhappy and had lost interest in both her appearance and the socialising she had previously enjoyed. Many of her friends had been younger than her and she was used to comments such as 'you've got so much energy for a ninety-three year old' and 'you're marvellous for your age!' She used to smile sweetly at these comments but actually found them rather irritating. As far as she was concerned it as not a matter of age itself, but of how she had lived her life, that had contributed most to her usual sprightliness. After a few more months her physical condition had improved, but she still felt despondent and apathetic. After some initial reluctance she was persuaded to take up the offer of a place at a day centre, in the hope that engaging with other people would make her feel better. It took all of her emotional reserves to make the effort to get herself ready and to face being introduced to all those new people. Her initial concerns began to recede when she was greeted by the day centre manager in a respectful and welcoming manner but resurfaced very quickly when a volunteer addressed her as 'poppet' and remarked on how 'cute' she looked with her tiny frame and Chinese dress. Only once during that first day was Mrs Leung referred to by her proper name, and then it was mispronounced. It only took one morning for her to come to the conclusion that the patronising and infantilising attitudes at this centre would do more harm to her than it would do good and to decide that her first day there would also be her last.

It is not uncommon for adolescents also be treated as if still children. That is, although they may have experienced a range of situations, including coping with change, and developed mature attitudes and open minds, they may still be conceptualised by some adults as incompetent to make decisions or inform discussions.

Medicalisation

This refers to the tendency for old age to be necessarily equated with sickness and the sick role. As mentioned earlier, there is undoubtedly an association between ageing and ill health but that does not justify the perception that old age itself is a sickness. One has only to think of people who have retained their health and vitality well into their old age to put paid to that myth but it is an extremely powerful and pervasive myth regardless of evidence to the contrary. Its power is such that it is taken on board by older people themselves, who often cope unnecessarily with disabling pain and immobility because they perceive these as 'symptoms' of old age rather than of a specific condition which has occurred as they have aged. This is an example of 'internalised oppression' whereby older people themselves come to believe that they are 'less than' others in society, an issue I will discuss in more detail later in Part One.

In terms of helping us to understand prevailing ideas and assumptions in particular sectors of the population, the concept of 'cohort effect' is a useful one. For example, the present cohort (or group of people who grew up within the same era) of people aged 80 or above will have experienced or witnessed the effects of a national strike, economic depression and World War II. They will have lived through a time when the National Health Service and the National Insurance scheme did not exist. The present cohort of people in their 40s or their 20s will have had very different experiences, which may well influence how they understand the world around them and what they expect of it. In terms of medicalisation, the experience of many older people will have been one of a relationship where the medical profession commanded respect and even deference, an attitude which they may well have carried with them into their old age and which can limit their expectations of a healthcare system which does not always give them a fair deal (Evans *et al.*, 2003).

The concept of power is a thread which has run through most of the discussions this far. We have seen how particular processes can bolster an image of dependency. In linking old age with 'the sick role' this unequal power relationship is compounded. While there have been some recent challenges to the power of the medical profession to 'call the tune', especially since the internet has opened up a lot of easily accessible information to the lay person, the medical profession still wield a lot of power and influence.

Marginalisation

This refers to the process of pushing people to the margins of society and of preventing or dissuading them from participating in mainstream activities. In essence it is about social exclusion.

As we have already seen, where older people are concerned, this is partly due to dominant social attitudes about older people's right to participate, but it is also about people having the means to participate in what is happening around them. Consider the following examples of how exclusion can occur:

- *High transport costs:* Becoming involved in one's community or visiting others to work, study or socialise often incurs financial costs. In some areas public transport for older people is subsidised, but this is not always the case and, of course, social exclusion affects younger people too. For example, feedback about the issues young people raised with the Children's Commissioner for Wales indicated that many feel excluded by the high admission costs to leisure facilities and the transport costs involved in getting access to them. Some perceive themselves as being discriminated against in the light of the free or subsidised transport being made available to older people in their localities (Masters, 2003).
- *Lack of suitable transport:* For many, especially those living in rural areas, public transport services are not effective or accessible. Without their own transport many have to either remain isolated or use expensive services such as private taxis.
- *Physical segregation:* While social policy over the last few decades has helped to reverse the trend of institutionalisation, it remains the case that many older people and, indeed, children and young people, live in residential settings. Budgetary restraints and the scarcity of specialist services often result in people being moved away from the communities they had previously lived in.
- *Media and peer pressure:* Children and young people can often feel excluded if their families cannot afford to buy them the clothes that are

currently fashionable, or fund the social activities that their friends engage in. At a time in their lives when they are often seeking peer approval to boost self-esteem, poverty may contribute towards social exclusion.

As we can see, it is not always a case of individuals seeking to exist outside of the mainstream, but that their situation is often a consequence of policies and strategies operating at the cultural and structural levels of discrimination.

Practice Focus 1.4

Callum was dreading the summer holidays again this year. Things weren't too bad before they moved to the new house. Where they lived before he was close to the city centre and so he could go the library or the museum, or wander around the shops to see what he could buy if only he had the money. But now that they had moved there was nothing for him to do. He was sure that no children had been consulted when the estate he now lived on had been designed because there were no open spaces where they could play without being called nuisances or asked to keep the noise down. Getting to the city centre cost a fortune on the train so that was out of the question now. He'd made new friends at school but they'd stopped calling round because he wasn't interested in playing computer games, which was all they seemed to do, and he didn't have any. And they could never understand why he didn't have a mobile phone so that they could text him. He used to pretend he'd lost his or let his mum borrow it, but the excuses were wearing thin and he was becoming a bit of a laughing stock because of it. He took to staying in bed for as long as he could, or watched television all day, but then he was always getting accused of being lazy and unimaginative. That really got to him because there was no shortage of enthusiasm or energy – he *wanted* to get involved in things but all of the courses, day schools and trips he saw advertised cost money and that was something that his family didn't have. He'd had to leave the football team when it became clear that he'd have to buy his own kit. By the end of the summer holidays he knew that his reputation as a reclusive and lazy young teenager would be even stronger and yet this seemed so unfair – that wasn't him at all.

Dehumanisation

Dehumanisation is about reducing people to the status of things or objects. It is about denying or taking away what it is that makes us people. As sentient beings we have feelings, hopes, fears and a myriad of other emotions and, although ageist ideology might suggest otherwise, these emotions do not suddenly spring into being once we reach the age of majority or cease when we reach pensionable age. Yet it is not uncommon for it to be assumed that this is the case.

One example is the assumption that neither older people nor children have a need to grieve. Moss and Moss (1989) have long pointed out that the majority of deaths are the deaths of older people and yet their experiences of grieving are not given a high profile in literature about dying and bereavement. Children and young people are also often treated as if they do not experience the same range of emotions as adults do when dealing with a variety of forms of loss, including divorce (Kroll, 2002) and foster care (Romaine, 2002) as well as the death of a loved one. The need to grieve is a very profound one and yet, as we can see, ageist ideology would have us believe that it only applies to those who are deemed to be 'real' adults. It is as if children and, to use a very apt term 'post-adults' (Midwinter, 1990), are not perceived as having the full range of emotions that define us as human. As I have suggested elsewhere (Thompson, 2002b) when referring to the management of grief in old age:

> If we continue to conceptualise the suffering . . . and to exclude them from the understanding and help that we would see as valid forms of intervention when working with younger bereaved or traumatised adults, then we run the risk of perpetuating what is, arguably, ageism's most demeaning process – dehumanisa- tion. If we accept that loss is indeed part of life, and we accept that older people are not a group apart from 'adults', then surely to deny the impact of loss and grief in their lives is to treat them as if they were already dead'. (p. 173)

In her discussion of dependency, Lustbader (1991) echoes this assumption that we become different beings on reaching old age. In focusing on reciprocity, or giving back, as something that defines us as human, she comments on a tendency to forget that people generally feel a need to be 'of use'. In the following passage she highlights the common practice in caregiving of denying this need:

> Frail people are generally denied chances to give something back to their helpers or to their communities. Their offers are refused with statements like, "You don't have to do that. We'll take care of everything". Helpers mean well, without realising how urgently people in their care crave a tangible counterpart to their dependency. (p. 29)

These are but two examples from many that could be included in a discussion of how human dignity, or rather the denial of it, can be justified on the grounds of age. You will probably be able to think of many more, and it is something we will return to in Part Two. One very basic human right is that of personal safety, and the prevalence of child and elder abuse suggests that this is not always being respected. As a manifestation of ageism, I would suggest that it merits a section in its own right.

Abuse

Abuse of both children and elders can be seen to operate in a number of forms, including physical, psychological, sexual, emotional and financial harm. Under- pinning all of these manifestations of abuse is the concept of power, or rather the abuse of power to the detriment of relatively powerless individuals or groups. That it happens to both young and old people suggests that the perpetrators rely on the ageist assumptions and processes we have already referred to. That is to say, they may well be influenced by messages around them to develop their own perceptions of these groups as having no need for protection, dignity or respect for feelings. As such it relies heavily on the dehumanisation process which ageist ideology so readily promotes.

Reports of abuse are often portrayed as the actions of individuals. You can probably recall accounts of children or older people being hit, starved, neglected or demeaned by uncaring or overstressed relatives or carers. But while this is not uncommon, we cannot always lay the blame fully at the door of individuals. Indeed, at the time of writing, the House of Lords is debating measures to regulate the prescription of anti-psychotic and other similar drugs to help prevent them being inappropriately used in the care of older people with dementia, a practice considered by some to be as abusive as restricting liberty by the use of physical restraint. If we remind ourselves of the cultural context in which individuals operate we can perhaps see how abuse comes to be regarded as reasonably acceptable in some circumstances. In a context where we constantly receive messages that old equals worthless and that children are too young to have earned respect, the foundations are laid for abuse to occur. And when those ideas are part and parcel of the fabric of society to the extent that they remain relatively unchallenged, the abuse of power goes relatively unchallenged too. Furthermore, we must not forget the effect of structural factors such as poverty, which can lead to tension and strain within families as they struggle to cope with competing demands on limited incomes.

It is true that child abuse has become the focus of a great deal of intellectual debate and there are major attempts to address it by means of legislation and policy directives, but it has to be borne in mind that it is only relatively recently in our history that child abuse has even been recognised as a concept to be addressed by society (Corby, 1989). In the case of elder abuse its recognition and validity as an issue to be dealt with is even more recent (Bennett *et al.*, 1997; Pritchard, 1994).

Internalisation of oppression

One of the features of ageist oppression is that it lowers self-esteem. If one is constantly picking up messages that older people are 'less than' others, then it becomes difficult not to take that to heart or 'internalise' it so that you come to believe it too. This helps to make ageist oppression even more potent than if it were just experienced objectively. We referred earlier to how the power of ideology relies heavily on its ability to ensure that its own particular beliefs or perspective become 'part of the wallpaper', so that they operate in the background without arousing comment or debate. This process can be seen to be operating effectively when comments such as the following are heard: 'I'll not bother the doctor about this chronic pain – it's just old age so I'll have to put up with it'; or, 'It's all I can expect at my age'; or, at the other end of the age spectrum: 'There's no point asking – they won't listen to me because I'm only a kid'.

An important consequence of internalising oppression is that it helps to quash any resistance from those on the receiving end of it. Of course, there will always be some resistance and there are many political and interest groups who are very vocal in their challenge to the ageist myth that older people should not be active in public life. However, this should not detract from the considerable effect that internalised oppression can have on people's confidence in their own abilities and the willingness of others to accept them as valuable members of the community. This comment by Lustbader (1991) is very apt in terms of a 'self-fulfilling prophecy':

> Deflecting disdain on so many levels at once takes considerable stamina. Instead, many older people absorb the contempt and begin to despise themselves for no longer being young. They shrink themselves down to the size of these degrading expectations, taking on the outer demeanour which constrains their self-expression but which is regarded by others as more acceptable for their age. (p. 119)

In the last few decades the user involvement movement (including those factions representing the interests of both younger and older people) has been gaining in strength as consumers of services have become more aware of their rights and look to ways of ensuring that their opinions are heard at the level of policy making and service delivery. This is something which will be discussed further in Part Two. But, while it is true that such groups are beginning to tackle age discrimination, the fact that *they* exist as a challenge is testament to the fact that *it* exists as a process.

Denial of citizenship rights

Citizenship is a huge area of study, but its main focus is on rights and responsibilities. In essence it is about what we should expect as citizens of a particular society and what is expected of us (for example, that we will obey the law). For our purposes here we will concentrate more closely on rights. These can include rights such as:

- being able to vote and have political representation;
- being provided with education and health care ;
- protection from physical harm or destitution; and
- the protection of property.

On the face of it, these rights would appear to be universally applied but, on closer inspection, it would seem that age is often used as an indicator of competence and worth. Many citizenship rights are conferred only when a child reaches the 'age of maturity', when they are felt to have earned that right. For example, a young person is not allowed political representation until he or she is 18 years old. At the other end of the spectrum there would also appear to be an element of 'worthiness' involved. While citizenship rights are not *actually* withdrawn on the grounds of age, at an ideological level they would appear to be given less recognition. Thompson (1992) uses the following example to illustrate this point:

> The negative and derogatory images of older people implicit in ageism have the effect of lowering expectations in respect of both rights and duties. For example, in terms of rights, it is often assumed by carers of elderly people that social services departments have the right to remove elderly people to care on a compulsory basis because they are 'at risk'. Contrary to the dominance of such a belief elderly people do have the right to remain in their own homes regardless of the degree of risk to which they are exposed . . . However, a right which is widely assumed not to exist is a severely weakened right. (p. 35)

Lowe (2003) makes a related point in highlighting that older people in the residential care system do not seem to be benefiting from the protection afforded others under recent human rights legislation. Ageist thinking can also be seen to underpin the lack of progress on addressing children's rights, given that it is only very recently that children's rights have been taken seriously enough to warrant specific government attention in the form of Children's Commissioners.

These have been just a small selection from a number of processes through which ageism can be seen to be operating. As we have seen, ageist ideology is very influential in terms of putting across ideas about how certain people *ought* to behave and be treated. In this final section of Part One, we will look at the validity of some of the more prevalent assumptions about older and younger people.

Life course expectations

As we have already discussed, ageist ideology promotes ideas about how certain age groups think and behave and, indeed, how they *should* think and behave. Ageism's power to oppress relies heavily on those value judgements being taken on board by a general population who fail to notice that these messages are influencing their thoughts and actions. This is not about laying the blame at the door of individuals, as it is only to be expected that we should fail to notice these ideas, assumptions, stereotypes and so on. It is when they become something we hear so much about that we begin to take them for granted as accepted 'truths' that these ideas are at their most potent – the dominant ideologies that were referred to earlier.

So let us move on to explore some of the assumptions that exist about older people and to explore the extent to which they are accurate or based on myth:

Older people choose to withdraw from society   One theoretical viewpoint which has been very influential in this respect in the past is that of disengagement theory (Cummings and Henry, 1961). From this perspective it is assumed that old age is necessarily a period of decline and that it is in the interests of society being able to function harmoniously that people move themselves to the margins of society as they age. This view gives credence to stereotypical images such as 'gran' sitting in her rocking chair, letting the world and its problems pass her by. One has only to think of the part that the Pensioners' Movement has played in the world of politics to see that old age can be a time for investing more time, rather than less, in the world around us. In a similar vein, many older people choose to continue working in paid employment, as volunteers and as carers and childminders, thereby making quite a considerable contribution to society rather than withdrawing from it. It also has to be said that, as major consumers of products and services such as those of the health and leisure industries, older people make a very significant contribution to the economy.

Older people are dependent   While it cannot be denied that there is a correlation between ageing and ill health, this is a far cry from claiming that old age *equates* with dependency. There are indeed older people who are dependent on others to a significant degree, but there is evidence to suggest that these are in the minority, as we have already seen. Furthermore, a considerable number of older people care not only for themselves but for others too. The census figures for 2001 indicate that there are more than 5.2 million carers in Britain, who regularly provide unpaid care to dependent relatives. Over a million regularly provide more than 50 hours of care per week and of these over half are aged over 55 years (source: www.statistics.gov.uk).

Older people aren't interested in learning   The University of the Third Age (u3a) is a registered charity which developed out of a recognition that many older people have both the desire and the skills to continue studying themselves and to facilitate studying by others in their age group. The fact that there are now 522 autonomous learning groups and a membership of over 130,000 older people suggests that this is indeed a myth, as does the number of older people undertaking courses of study with the Open University.

Older people have poor memories   A pervasive stereotype of an older person is one who is either forgetful or confused and there is often an assumption that ageing and dementia are one and the same thing. Dementia *is* a feature of old age and a significant number of older people do develop it. Department of Health figures from 2001 suggest that the number of sufferers in Britain is somewhere around 600,000. However, given the overall population of older people in Britain, it is clear that the vast majority are *not* suffering from it. As noted earlier, many older people retain their intellectual capacities to the extent that they continue to engage in undergraduate and postgraduate study, run businesses, hold senior positions in central and local government and so on.

Older people are resistant to change One image of old age that crops up regularly in the forms of jokes and the like is that of the person who thrives on nostalgia and constantly harks back to 'the good old days'. One has only to look at the extent to which advances in technology such as the Internet have been taken on board and used to great effect by older people, to counter that myth. The Age Concern website (see Part Four) provides figures to suggest that, in 2002, 14 per cent of people over 65 years had used the internet, and 25 per cent of two-adult households (where one or both were over 60 years) owned a home computer.

Older people are just old Perhaps one of the most devastating features of ageist ideology is its power to hide the individual in all of his or her complexity under the blanket reference 'old', as if the other aspects of one's identity cease to be of importance when one reaches old age. If we think about what contributes to our being who we are (our class, colour, religion, sexual orientation, interests and housing status to name but a few) it is clearly ridiculous to assume that these will automatically change or cease to be of relevance on reaching a pre-determined date and yet this is what is often assumed. For example, someone with Down's Syndrome is increasingly likely to experience old age with that condition and yet, as Grant (2001) points out, older people with learning disabilities tend not to be offered therapeutic interventions or have their needs researched to the extent that younger learning-disabled people do. In old age, people from ethnic minorities continue to experience the same forms of discrimination that they have experienced prior to that point and yet this is not often taken on board. Clegg, (2003) and Zarb (1993) comment that people with congenital or acquired physical disabilities are likely to experience old age with those disabilities and yet tend to become classified as 'old' rather than disabled on reaching 60 or 65 years. In Part Three we will look in more detail at how ageism interacts with other forms of discrimination, but something to bear in mind at this point is how thinking about old people as just 'old' can also serve to make other aspects of their identity fade into the background so that they are unlikely to be addressed.

We can now explore some assumptions about children and young people:

Children and young people are lazy Baldwin and Hirst (2002) make the point that as many as 50,000 young people are heavily involved in caring for a sick or disabled family member, with one in ten young carers looking after one or more dependent people. This can include domestic duties in addition to providing personal care. Given that some families may not report this situation, this figure may be an underestimation. Even so, it provides a challenge to the stereotype of children and young people as lazy. And, while recent reports in the media focus on the supposedly increasing tendency for children and young people to have sedentary lifestyles, this is not true of all. Many regularly take part in sporting activities, and to a high standard. In fields such as swimming, ice-skating and athletics, many spend hours each day on rigorous training programmes, as well as attending school full-time.

Children and young people are only interested in themselves   One has only to visit the websites of charities and voluntary agencies to note that many of them celebrate the participation of children and young people. For example, Voluntary Service Overseas has a thriving youth programme, which aims to promote understanding between different cultures and involves young people in work that benefits the countries involved in their programmes. The high level of support given by young people to charities and other organisations involved in such fields as animal welfare and protection of the environment, suggests that this accusation of self-centredness is often undeserved.

Practice Focus 1.5

Craig and Shamila had been so disappointed to see their train leaving the station that they slumped to the floor of the waiting room. They were wet, hungry and dishevelled and realised that they must look quite a sight for sore eyes. They had run right across the town in the hope of catching the train, because there would not be another one for over two hours. Once they had caught their breath they began to see the funny side of things and collapsed on to each other's shoulders in fits of laughter. At this point a man joined them in the waiting room and stared at them until they began to feel uncomfortable. Another passenger joined them and she too looked in their direction with a disapproving expression. Before long the two adults were talking about them as if they weren't there, making remarks about their appearance and 'rowdy' behaviour. The man commented that it was typical of young people to be lazing about like that and the woman agreed with him. Craig and Shamila felt hurt by these accusations and wondered whether they ought to mention that they had just been dropped off in the town after completing a 25-mile charity walk in atrocious weather conditions. They looked at each other and decided not to. They were just too tired to challenge such pre-judging and, anyway, they had their own warm glow of pride which would keep them going until they could reach their respective homes and sink into a lovely hot bath.

Children and young people are healthy   Although chronic ill health, disability and frailty are more often associated with the end of life than the beginning, many children have conditions which can seriously affect their quality of life. For example, arthritis is commonly associated with old age, but it is also a condition of childhood (Chronic Juvenile Arthritis) as too are debilitating conditions such as muscular dystrophy and cystic fibrosis.

Children and young people are resilient   Quilgars (2002) suggests that there has been an overall rise in the number of children and young people experiencing mental health problems since the middle of the 20th century and cites, amongst others:

- emotional disorders, such as depression;
- eating disorders; and

- conduct disorders, such as anti-social behaviour.

In the same edited collection Searle alerts us to the fact that, while the number of suicides by young people fell in the 1990s, suicide still accounted for one fifth of all deaths of young people in Britain. An indication of the stress that children and young people feel can be drawn from the fact that 'Childline', the national helpline specifically for this age group, receives over 4000 calls a day. While children can be seen to be resilient in some ways (Gilligan, 1997), it is important that this should not be overestimated.

Children and young people don't experience grief   People have loss experiences over a vast range of situations, including the death of a relative or friend, loss of loved ones through separation or divorce, and the loss of aspirations caused by accident or ill health, to name but a few. These are experienced by children too but are not always recognised as such, or responded to in a manner that is appropriate to their level of understanding. Doka (1995) echoes this point in the following extract from his preface to an edited collection of papers about children's mourning:

> Throughout the field of death studies, there has been a recurring debate over whether children reach a level of developmental maturity when they are capable of recognising and experiencing loss. To many, the answer is that children at any age can recognise loss though they may respond to it in different ways. (p. xii)

But Doka also asks us to think about the similarities between adults' and children's mourning, as well as the differences:

> Like adults, each loss is different. The grief experience will be affected by many of the same factors that affect adults – the nature and quality of the relationships, the availability of support, the circumstances of the loss, the psychological resilience and coping skills of the child, as well as social variables such as class, gender, religion and culture. (ibid.)

There is a wide range of support and advice available to those experiencing grief reactions to a whole host of loss situations. Ageism can be seen to be operating when this support is denied on the grounds of age.

Conclusion

Recognising the existence of ageism is the first step towards challenging it and so, to that end, the discussions in Part One have focused on its theoretical underpinnings. In exploring some of ageism's complexities, including how it operates at different levels and through different processes, it has become clear that to focus on the level of individual prejudice is to miss the significance that cultural and structural factors can also play in perpetuating disadvantage. The concept of stereotyping has featured strongly because it operates at the level of ideas to influence our perceptions of the worth of people around us. In the previous section, some of those negative stereotypical images of young people and people in their old age have been undermined, and this will hopefully lead you to further question the origin of popular images and reflect on whether they have any basis in reality.

By heightening your awareness of the extent and power of ageist ideology it is to be hoped that you will want to play a part in challenging ageism where you can see it operating. With that in mind, let us turn to the implications for practice.

Introduction

In Part One we explored the theoretical underpinnings of age discrimination in order to give us a better understanding of what it is and how it operates. It is to be hoped that you will have taken on board that ageism is a powerful and complex force which can lead to significant sections of the population being disadvantaged in a number of ways and at a number of levels. Up to this point the discussion has been at a general theoretical level but in Part Two the focus will move to consider the implications of that theorising for practice, in whatever form it might take.

Within the confines of this book, and indeed any other, it would be impossible to cover every set of circumstances in which people work with older people or children and young people, and so what follows will inevitably be a selective overview. What is required of you as you read through this section, is that you consider what anti-ageist practice would look like within your own particular workplace or practice situation and to use what follows as a guide or a springboard for generating ideas about how you can challenge ageist assumptions and practices and how you can help to ensure that your own practice is based on anti-ageist principles.

As noted, it is all too easy to rely on ideas we have in our heads about typical behaviours, attitudes and lifestyles in certain sectors of the population and to let the assumptions we make about their needs and aspirations operate as a short cut to providing support or services. What these generalisations fail to do is to recognise the enormous variation which occurs within any group of people who are defined by one characteristic only. Seniors Network, an organisation which provides an information source to older people, claims that out of a total population of almost 60 million people in Britain, more than 10.7 million are aged 65 and older. And, according to the most recent census figures, there are approximately 12 million children under 16 years. As we have already discussed, it is clearly ridiculous to think that those populations will not be differentiated in a variety of other respects. For example, any two people in their 80s could be as different as chalk and cheese in terms of gender, ethnic origin, class background, sexual orientation, career profile, marital status and religious affiliation to name but a few. Every single one of those aspects of his or her existence will have an enormous impact on their identity and life experience and yet ageist stereotyping works in such a way that those vitally important aspects are hidden under a blanket categorisation by age alone. And, of course, this is equally true of children and young people.

So, if acting on stereotypes leads us dangerously close to the pitfalls of ageist practice, how can we ensure that our own practice is *anti*-ageist practice? How can we be sure that our practice challenges, rather than reinforces, those stereotypes? The guidance which follows is not intended to be comprehensive. Nor will it necessarily answer the particular dilemmas that your own practice situations might throw up. You will not find 'off the peg' solutions here, because anti-ageist practice argues for individually tailored responses and an approach based on practice that is reflective. This is something that is discussed in detail by authors such as Schön (1983), and Thompson (2000) but, in a nutshell, reflective practice is about having a questioning and evaluative approach to what you do, so that your practice is not based on knee-jerk reactions or carried out in a particular way because 'that's the way it has always been done'. It is about practice being *informed* practice – that is to say practice that is underpinned by, for example:

- a value base;
- a knowledge base; and
- a research base,

which feed into how and why we do what we do, and requires us to evaluate our work.

Given that such a practice is the opposite of a 'one size fits all approach' it would be inappropriate, and indeed impossible, for me to offer practice solutions without knowing what the practice problems are. Instead, what follows are some practice guidelines which I feel will be broadly applicable to many situations. They should serve to give you food for thought in terms of promoting anti-ageist practice. As you read through them, and the practice examples which accompany them, try to relate them to the particular field in which you work.

Listen to people

We have talked a lot about stereotypes and the tendency to assume that we know what children, young people and older people are like and what they will want or need in the way of services and support. A key issue here, if we are to resist falling into the trap of using age alone as an indicator of behaviour and need, is the need to listen to people. Without listening to individuals we cannot hope to build up a picture of what goes into making them who they are, where they are coming from and who and where they want to be, and yet there are numerous examples of situations where this does not happen. The actual process of listening is one that seems, on the face of it, to be a very simple activity. However, it is a much more complex skill than it might first seem. For example, how we listen is related to what the purpose of our listening is and, if we are not careful, we can lose sight of the need to focus very particularly on giving people the time and 'permission' to get their view across. There are many distractions that can get in the way of this aim, including the following selection from those identified by McKay *et al.* (1995):

- *rehearsing:* thinking ahead about one's own responses instead of concentrating on what is being said.
- *filtering:* being selective about which bits are heard and which are allowed to blur into the background.
- *judging:* having preconceptions about the worth of what someone else has to say.
- *dreaming:* allowing one's thoughts to wander, so that concentration on what is being said is lost.
- *advising:* allowing oneself to be thinking of how to help rather than concentrating on how the problem is being defined from the other person's perspective.

These are but a few of those covered, but should be enough to remind us of how much thought needs to be given to the process of listening if it is to be effective. It is an important issue in terms of anti-ageist practice and so I would refer you to the suggestions for further reading in Part Four. However, given that this is such a broad topic, and that space permits only a very quick skim over the surface, for the purposes of this discussion about ageism, we will move on to concentrate more on the *why* of listening than the *how*. So, in terms of anti-ageist practice, listening is crucial because:

It gives us a perspective on how other people define the problem to be addressed.

In order for us to be able to help address a problem or need, we first have to identify what it is that we are trying to achieve. We have to work through the process of 'problem setting', which calls into question who it is that does the defining. Given the typical image of older people as dependent and incapable, it is not unusual for workers to assume that they themselves need to take responsibility for defining the problem and facilitating what they perceive to be the appropriate response. For example, if we look at the provision of care services for older people, there is sometimes a tendency for day-centre and residential or nursing home activities programmes to be organised around assumptions that *all* older people enjoy the relatively popular pursuits of bingo, old-time sing-songs and watching television. Although there is usually a choice about whether to participate or not, it is often the case that the activities themselves are chosen by the person organising the activities programme, rather than by the people who are expected to take part. This can result in a 'take it or leave it' approach and those who choose to take the latter option can all too often be labelled as unsociable or withdrawn, when the real issue is that the social activities on offer would never have interested them in their earlier lives and continue to have little appeal in old age. Taking a *person*-led approach rather than a *system*-led one would provide the opportunity for a more individualised approach that relies less on assumptions about how older people *should* be occupying their time and more on how they *want* to do so.

Practice Focus 2.1

Alf's bungalow was full of memorabilia about the regiment he had served with during a long military career and of photographs of comrades, some of whom were long since dead and others with whom he kept in contact on a regular basis. Alf's capacity to look after himself had been adversely affected by a series of strokes which had left him physically weak but had not affected his memory or speech. Although he tended to get depressed at times, what kept his spirits up was his weekly visit to the local Ex-Servicemen's Club. Only something really serious like being admitted to hospital would put a stop to his weekly meeting with friends, and his helpers knew better than to think even bad weather would deter him, such was his need to keep up this aspect of his social life.

When a fourth stroke made it too difficult for him to continue living at home, Alf reluctantly agreed to move into residential care. After a month he was asked whether he felt he had made the right decision. He answered that he felt that the physical care he received was second to none, but one thing was making him unhappy. He didn't feel as if the staff knew him as a person – if they did, then they would stop trying to interest him in the social activities on offer there. For the last 20 years he had spent his days listening to news and sport on the radio and, as far as he was concerned, he could continue doing that in his room to his own timetable. What bothered him most of all was the feeling that he was expected to fit with what other people thought he might like. He *liked* to spend time on his own with his books and photograph albums, so why keep trying to drag him away from it? And was it too much to ask that his Friday night out be able to continue if he had people willing to help him? He felt he had lost enough already – was it necessary to lose that too? Alf felt comfortable and safe in his new home, but he was beginning to feel that he didn't know who he was any more and that frightened him.

It helps to make assessment processes more holistic. It is all too easy to focus inadvertently on a particular aspect of a person's situation, ability or whatever, at the expense of others that may not be quite so obvious. This is often because our own work environment or personal experience leads us to attach more significance to those aspects which have a direct bearing on what we are trying to achieve. For example, if we are involved in planning hospital discharges, it may be a person's physical ability that is the prime focus of an assessment process.

Someone working in the victim support field may perhaps have a stronger focus on emotional than physical needs. Those working in housing and education will probably have those particular needs higher on their agenda than others. This is not to say that this will be to the total exclusion of other aspects and it is not my intention to be critical of any particular profession. I merely wish to suggest that, with a myriad of aspects to consider, it is not surprising that some may be overlooked or their significance downplayed.

This is where listening becomes crucial. Without hearing the perspective of the younger or older person, our own biases are likely to come into play and we may then miss something that is of immense significance to them but not obvious to us. For example, it may be extremely important to a frail older man that he has access to a mosque, but this might be overlooked by a relative or worker trying to persuade him to move to live with his son in another part of the city because of concerns about his physical well-being. The significance of this to him may never become apparent without listening to him and inviting his perspective. Similarly, a child's need to maintain a connection with a dead grandmother by visiting her grave may not be apparent to someone arranging an emergency foster care placement. But to that particular child, in those particular circumstances of change and uncertainty, that particular need may eclipse all others.

As we have already discussed, ageist ideology tempts us to take short cuts by working on the assumption that all people of a certain age are broadly similar and that the views of children and older people are of less importance than those of 'real' adults. Taking the time out to listen helps to counteract this by reminding us that our perspectives, values and life views are not the only ones that matter. *It lets people know they are valued.* To ignore others' perspectives and rely on our own assumptions is to send out the message 'your views are worthless – I won't even bother listening to you'. To some degree this can be explained by a tendency towards paternalism and a desire to protect. It is often assumed that children and young people are too naive to look after their own interests and that decisions are best left to those with the wisdom and expertise that age is supposed to bring. And where older people are conceptualised *en masse* as frail and confused, it is all too often seen as one's duty to ensure that they are protected from risk, such as living in houses that are in poor repair, or not following guidelines on healthy eating. While this desire to protect is, in many ways, an admirable one, it has to be balanced with a respect for rights if it is not to be oppressive.

We all make decisions based on risk taking. For example, we know that it is possible that we may be involved in a road accident if we leave the house, but few of us stay indoors because of that. Some people take part in extreme sports because it meets a need for excitement and personal challenge, even though they know that there is a relatively high risk of injury. While others may not agree with the choices we make, we expect them to respect our right to do so, as it indicates respect for our competence in making judgements. When a paternalistic approach is applied across the board, purely on age grounds, it assumes a lack of competence across the board. Listening to individuals can help to challenge this by highlighting difference, and showing that competence is not necessarily age related.

Given that listening is so crucial it is worth giving some thought to how effective listening can best be facilitated. Listening relies on people first having the opportunity for their voice to be heard. We will explore how this can be achieved at a group level later in Part Two but, at an individual level, this means ensuring that the timing and setting are conducive and that individuals are given the opportunity to communicate in a way, and at a pace that suits them. For some who have difficulty in expressing themselves in words, such as very young children, people with learning difficulties and those with dementing conditions, it may be necessary to 'listen' in different ways – observing body language and mood change, or with the use of pictures or symbols (Barnett, 2000; Woolf and Woolf, 2003). An anti-ageist approach requires us to work in partnership with the people concerned, and it is difficult to see how that can be done without listening. This is not necessarily easy in every circumstance, but that does not mean that this important principle should be abandoned.

Exercise 2.1

Listening to people and hearing what they say is not always successfully carried out. What barriers to effective listening can you identify when working with:

    (a) children?

    (b) young people?

    (c) older people?

How can you help to make sure that these perspectives are heard?

Listening is always important in people work of any type as it forms a basis on which partnership working can flourish. It is perhaps particularly so when working with those whose wishes and life chances are so often compromised by ageist assumptions and preconceptions. Nevertheless, it is only one component of effective communication and so let us consider the bigger picture.

Make communication work

For communication to work well it has to be understood by both sides, the person sending the message and the person receiving it. This sounds so basic that it should hardly need saying. And yet it is so often the case that something goes wrong in that process, with the result that communication is misinterpreted or does not even reach its intended recipient.

As Thompson (2003) comments:

Perhaps it is because language is so important and such an ingrained part of our everyday life that it is very common for people to take it for granted and not realize just how significant a role it plays. We should also be aware that language is a very complex phenomenon, and it is not uncommon for people to oversimplify it. This is no doubt also due to its familiarity. (p. 37)

Because it is something we do every day in one form or another, it is not surprising that we feel we just need to let the words come out of our mouths, make our signs or whichever form of communication we use, and the meaning will be clear. However, it is easy to forget that language takes place within a context or a number of contexts. For example, the gender of the speaker or the recipient can affect the interaction, as too can the cultural background and the social standing of either or both (see Thompson, 2003, and Cameron, 1998, for a more detailed discussion of these issues). While effective communication is crucial to anti-ageist practice it is far too complex a topic to go into in any depth in an introductory book such as this and I would urge you to look at the suggested reading in Part Four. Whether you follow this up or not, the main point to take on board is that effective people work requires that we develop a heightened awareness of what is going on when we are communicating. With that awareness we are more likely to avoid the pitfalls that prevent effective communication from happening. Anti-ageist practice involves working hard to ensure that this happens with everyone, and relies on our valuing people at both ends of the age spectrum enough to make that effort.

So what can help to make communication effective? The following list of suggestions is not comprehensive but should get you thinking about how you can help to ensure that your practice challenges, rather than reinforces, ageism.

Verbal communication

- Do ensure that what you say has been understood. Asking the person you have been speaking with to reflect back their understanding of the main points is one way of ensuring that the message has got across. Don't assume that your message has been understood in the way it was intended by you. Remember that the other person is not inside your head with you and may interpret what you are saying differently from you, especially given that words and concepts tend to be attributed with different meanings in different eras.
- Do take into account that others may not understand terms or concepts with which you yourself are familiar, for example professional jargon or technical terms. This puts the other person at an unfair disadvantage and people may feel embarrassed and belittled at having to ask for clarification.
- Don't just repeat things in the same manner if people look bewildered. The problem may lie with your delivery of the message rather than with the

recipient. Step back and analyse whether you would understand if you were in the other person's shoes, without your knowledge, perspective and so on.

- Do make allowances for any disabling conditions which might be present, such as hearing impairments and speech difficulties, such as those associated with strokes or conditions like Parkinson's Disease. While not necessarily specific to old age, conditions which impact on the ability to communicate are not uncommon in the later stages of life and care needs to be taken that each particular difficulty is understood and addressed.

- Don't assume that all communication difficulties can be addressed by raising one's voice or speaking more slowly. This is rarely effective and often makes things more difficult.

- Do ensure that account is taken of the other person's level of understanding or stage of development. While it is true that some older people's understanding becomes impaired because of dementia or other conditions associated with ageing, there is as wide a range of intellectual ability across the spectrum of people in old age as at any other stage of life. It can be patronising to be spoken to as if one is stupid, and it can be disempowering to be spoken to at a level that is beyond one's understanding. Where children are concerned, emotional maturity needs to be considered along-side actual chronological age if communication and consultation are not to be tokenistic.

- Do use a tone of speech that is appropriate to the occasion. There should be no justification for speaking to an older person or indeed a child or young person in a way that is disrespectful or patronising when the rationale is based on age alone. Although ageist ideology might suggest otherwise, we all have feelings whatever our age.

- Don't underestimate the effect of emotion on effective communication. When difficult or frightening topics are being discussed, as is often the case in people work, it often becomes difficult to concentrate on detail or to process and remember what is being said. Giving the opportunity for the process to be repeated or providing a written record may help ensure that the message gets across when heightened emotions come into the equation.

- Don't assume there will be a problem. Communication problems are not inevitable by any means. You are communicating with a person not a stereotype.

Practice Focus 2.2

Miss McGann had made an appointment to see someone at her local housing office. She would normally have gone on her own but a recent ear infection had left her with some temporary problems with her balance and so she had asked her nephew to accompany her just in case she should have an attack of dizziness. Having been a company director until her retirement eight years previously she had excellent planning skills and had prepared a list of questions for which she needed answers. She was prepared for the fact that the housing officer might not have the information she was looking for. What she was unprepared for was the officer's poor communication skills and ageist assumptions.

On entering the room she was surprised and offended when, after a very cursory nod in her direction, the officer directed all further conversation to Miss McGann's nephew, despite his protestations that he knew nothing of the actual reason for his aunt's request for a meeting. When she did manage to get a word in and insist that she be allowed the courtesy of being listened to, Miss McGann found that the officer raised her voice considerably when speaking to her, which was not only unnecessary, but also hurt her ears in their delicate state. She also had a tendency to talk over her, which meant that she often 'hijacked' the conversation to her own agenda. By focusing on what she thought the important issues were, the officer was failing to hear what was being said. She was so used to interviewing older people who wanted to move into smaller or more accessible accommodation that she assumed this was the reason for this visit and was already trying to access the housing availability data as Miss McGann was talking. The astute Miss McGann was able to see what she was doing and asked what relevance such data had to her wish to change the nature of her housing tenure so that she could offer board and lodgings to young homeless people.

The housing officer was taken aback at first but, on reflection, realised that she had allowed her assumptions about older people and their capabilities to get in the way of the listening and assessment skills that were crucially important in her field of work.

Written communication

Whatever your field of work, it is likely that your thoughts and actions will need to be recorded. Written communication is therefore an important component of any form of work with people. Some may need to write more often and in more depth than others, but the same principles of good anti-ageist practice apply whatever the context. Poor communication has often been cited as a key issue where practice has been found to be ineffective or dangerous (O'Rourke, 2002; Hopkins 2002a, 2002b) and poor or non-existent written communication suggests a lack of commitment to promoting high-quality practice. Most work with vulnerable people at either end of the age spectrum involves co-operation between individuals and agencies, which makes communication the lynchpin around which everything else revolves. An 'anything goes' attitude indicates a lack of interest and respect, and so the anti-ageist challenge relies on a commitment to ensuring that nobody (particularly where age is used as a justification) is on the receiving end of such an approach. So, what are the principles of effective recording? This is another huge topic and, again, one which you may wish to explore further. What follows are just a few of what I consider to be the most important in terms of ageism and anti-ageist practice:

- Do consider message taking as an important task. If messages are not taken seriously or recorded properly, then disastrous consequences can follow. It is all too easy to forget what may seem to be a small and insignificant task, or to fail to recognise the implications of that message not reaching its intended recipient. In these days of Internet access and mobile phones, many older people and children have less need to rely on others to pass messages on but there will still be many vulnerable people who do. It may seem like a task which requires little thought or attention, but vital information is often lost in the process of transmitting what one person is conveying and what someone else reads. For example, what is often lost in the process of transferring messages is clarity about *when* the message was taken, so that the recipient does not have the necessary information on which to judge how urgently the message needs to be responded to.

- Do keep your recording focused. If important information is to be conveyed it has to be presented in a format that is clear and focused, so that the reader does not have to wade through a mass of irrelevant detail in order to get to the nub of the report or instruction. That is, the recording style has to fit the purpose. It may be the case in one situation that a lot of specific detail is required whereas, in another, this detail would be superfluous. For example, written details in a daily logbook about the timing and contents of someone's meal may be crucial information for someone providing homecare to an older person with a condition such as diabetes. Similarly, leaving something crucial out (such as that someone with a learning disability is also deaf) can result in this not being picked up by someone who comes into contact with that person in an emergency situation, such as police intervention or an unplanned hospital admission. In other situations this amount of detail can be unnecessary or even intrusive.

- Don't rely on memory or verbal instructions, especially when several people are involved in addressing a problem. For example, following a meeting, an action plan which details who has agreed to take responsibility for particular issues, and to what timescale, can help to prevent a situation where things are either duplicated or forgotten about. Ensuring that older people and children are not left 'out of the loop' in this respect is a principle of anti-ageist practice.

- Do consider confidentiality. The ageist assumption that the feelings of young people and older people can be dispensed with as irrelevant can lead to issues of confidentiality being overlooked in some cases. Especially where someone is considered to be vulnerable in some way, it is not unusual for quite a number of people to be involved in service users' lives (district nurses, police officers, doctors, social workers, support or project workers, advocates, teachers and so on). On a practical level the sharing of information can be beneficial and, indeed, the concept of a 'unified assessment tool' is something that is high on the agenda of the bodies governing health and social care provision. However, this consideration should not·be allowed to override the right of citizens to have confidentiality respected.

- Do promote anti-ageist practice throughout whole organisations by enshrining principles in the form of written policies. These can help to make an organisation's values, strategies and practice guidelines clear to all involved and also act as a model of good practice to other organisations. The efforts of individuals can play a major part in challenging ageism, but changes at the level of organisational culture can have an even greater impact.

Practice Focus 2.3

Ada had been a volunteer at the social club for several months when she noticed that there was a tendency for the furniture to be rearranged in readiness for the twice weekly afternoon club for older residents of the village. Without fail, Ada would arrive on the designated days to find the chairs arranged around the walls and the tables stacked away in the corner. Ada realised that it would never be possible to recreate the cosiness of a sitting room in such a large building but felt that a more inviting and less impersonal atmosphere would be easy to create with a bit of imagination. She would move a few chairs around to create informal groups and encouraged the older visitors to do the same. However, on each new day, the chairs were always back around the walls and the tables put away. When she asked other volunteers about this, she was told that this was the way it had always been done and that they had followed the instructions of those who had been there before them. Surprised by this response she wondered how much of a say the older people had in this. There was no reason why they shouldn't, as far as Ada could see. After all, the chairs weren't bolted down and, if it made chatting and socialising difficult, then why continue with this arrangement? And so Ada carried on doing her bit to challenge the stereotype of older people as inactive and opinionless by encouraging them to set up smaller groups based on shared interests and particular friendships.

Before long she decided that she should do more than just 'plough her own furrow'. She spent some time researching user involvement initiatives and put together a short report on her findings, which she sent to the management committee. They were interested to hear her ideas and invited her to talk them through further. On reflection, they decided that the first step had to be one of consulting with those who used the club and, as it was due to be refurbished, felt that it was the perfect time to do so. They had planned to repaint the walls and replace the carpet but the overwhelming response of the service users was that the money would be better spent on having the facility to divide the large room off into smaller units, where they could engage in different activities. Eventually they came to a compromise but, as far as Ada was concerned, the most important development was that the management committee had changed its constitution so that, from that point on, it included a representative from amongst the club's users. From Ada's intervention, albeit on a small scale, the culture of the organisation had begun to change in a very significant way, and of that she was very proud.

Language has been a major feature of the preceding discussions, be it verbal or non-verbal, but one point that must not be overlooked in terms of anti-ageist practice is the *power* of language. This is a subject that is worth exploring in its own right.

Recognise language as a force for change

So far, language has been mentioned in general terms, as part of a wider discussion about the effectiveness of communication. But, more specifically, it can be seen as a vehicle for the transmitting of ideas and values, and an extremely powerful one because it is something which pervades our daily lives in one form or another. Language is used to describe and explain, to conjure up images and to influence our thinking in particular ways. This is particularly effective when it is used in subtle ways that influence us without most people being aware of what is happening. For example, in a newspaper article about ageism in recruitment adverts, Hughes (2003) refers to how The Employers' Forum on Age has highlighted that employers sometimes use words such as 'lively' when hoping to recruit someone young, and 'dependable' when trying to attract older applicants. Whilst not discriminating overtly, they nevertheless use language selectively to the same effect. And so, if we are in the business of trying to change entrenched ideas, then language use is something we need to think carefully about.

In a discussion about media power, McCullagh (2002) makes the following comment:

> many media sociologists argue that the source of media power lies in its ability to be selective in what it tells us about the world. It tells us about some issues and events and not about others. Thus it controls the information that is available to media audiences and so has the potential to shape or to set limits to their social knowledge and to the images that they can construct of the world in which they live. (p. 22)

In a similar way to 'media selectivity', the use of particular age-related terms can contribute to the images that we have about the world in which we live. For example, if negative derogatory labels such as 'brat' are routinely attached to young people and 'fogey' and 'codger' to older people, then their use perpetuates a negative image of these stages of life. As with media selectivity, the words chosen can give us only a partial picture of the world but suggest to us that it is the whole picture. In his poem, *White Comedy* (cited in Bulmer and Solomos, 1999), Benjamin Zephaniah writes about how black people have to cope with the constant association between blackness and negativity in the language they hear around them. Similarly, older people and teenagers who constantly hear and see images of themselves as nuisances may come to see that as 'how things are'. The following comments by Masters (2003), following an interview with the Children's Commissioner for Wales, puts this point over well:

> What has also surprised him is how widely young people share this view about lack of respect. 'It's obvious that this sort of drip feed of people who ring up phone-ins about smacking children and the way the media treats them and juvenile justice, that the general attitude really gets through to them and they have this feeling that they are seen as trouble'. (p. 8)

Many would argue that to worry about terminology is petty, and this has not been helped by examples of people trying to 'ban' the use of certain words, without an understanding of why they are considered to be problematic. For example, there have been attempts to ban the use of terms such as 'blackboard' and 'black coffee', on the grounds that they may cause offence. Such attempts appear to miss the point that it is the association between blackness and dirtiness, negativity or evil (such as in the terms 'black day', 'black mark' or 'black sheep') that is at issue, not the blackness per se. Thompson (2003) echoes this lack of understanding in the following passage:

> One of the main failings of the oversimplified political correctness approach to these issues is that it has not taken account of the need to change meanings rather than simply words. Its proponents have failed to take on board the subtlety and sophistication of language and communication and have thus relied on the naive assumption that promoting forms of language more consistent with equality and diversity is simply a matter of banning certain words and using certain others in their place. (p. 117)

He asks us to move on from either:

- dismissing language issues as unimportant, or
- trivialising and dismissing them as 'political correctness',

by thinking about these matters in terms of language *sensitivity*. That is, we should ask ourselves whether the terminology we use contributes to the construction of a negative image and whether we could use alternatives which are either neutral or help construct a positive image. For example, let us revisit two of the ageist processes that were flagged up in Part One:

Infantilisation The use of words such as 'sweetie' or 'pet', when used with reference to older people, has a negative and demeaning association which displays an indication of how the user sees the relationship between him or herself and the older person, that is one akin to a parent-child relationship. This is a value judgement which is harmful to the cause of anti-ageism and could be avoided by using the person's preferred name. The latter form of address promotes a positive image of someone who has retained their status and identity, the former terms do the opposite.

Dehumanisation An example of the power of language to oppress is when the term 'geriatric' is used as a noun, thereby reducing a person to an object or thing. It may seem like a harmless short-cut in terms of language use but, again, it sends out a very clear message about a lack of respect for individuality and identity. Once again, using a person's name would promote a much more positive image about respect and worth.

The power of language to oppress or, indeed challenge oppression, is a huge topic, and it is not possible to do it justice in such an introductory volume as this. For that reason I would urge you to give it more thought and to read further around the subject. But, before moving on to discuss change management more generally, here are some pointers for anti-ageist practice in terms of language use:

- Be sensitive to the power of words to convey meaning. Don't get so hung up that you are afraid to speak, but work on heightening your awareness of the messages you are putting across by the choice of terms you use. Discussing this in a group can be helpful in terms of finding alternative, and more neutral, terms to replace ones which you highlight as discriminatory.
- Move this analysis on by thinking about whether the agencies in which you work, or of which you have knowledge, convey ageist or anti-ageist messages. For example, the name of a team or organisation can give a clue to the values that underpin it.
- Challenge the insensitive use of demeaning terms by other people. I am not advocating a confrontational approach, but a more subtle one designed to get language sensitivity on other people's agendas too.
- Challenge the use of demeaning terms by older people and children themselves. Internalised ageism, as we referred to in Part One, can lead to low self-esteem and a negative self-image, and so those who are most affected by language insensitivity can play a part in perpetuating its use.
- Don't act on instructions about changing language use unless you can see its justification. Some organisations advise against the use of certain words but, if you can't see why a term has been 'banned' or substituted, then check it out. Sometimes the advice giving is born of a fear of being *accused* of discrimination, rather than of an *understanding* of discrimination.

> ### Exercise 2.2
>
> Pick an organisation that relates either to children and young people, or to older people. This may be the one you work within, or you may choose to explore a different one. Look at the terminology used in promotional material such as leaflets and websites. What does the language used convey about the organisation's values and how its users are perceived? Can you identify anything that either reinforces or challenges ageism?

As we have seen, giving thought to how we communicate can play a vital role in challenging the often unequal relationship between vulnerable people and those who work and interact with them. In the following section, we explore the role that the user involvement movement has and can play in challenging ageist assumptions and practices.

Challenge the power imbalance

If we are to have any commitment to anti-ageist practice, then good communication is just the starting point. Of course it is a vitally important starting point but also a complete waste of time if what is heard is not processed and acted on. By their very definition dialogues have more than one process going on. Those who are invited to, or choose to, enter into discussions rarely want the process to stop there, and so information is digested, analysed and an appropriate response is made. Or at least this is what should happen if both or all parties are to be satisfied with the process. What often happens as a result of ageist stereotyping is that it is assumed that those at the extremes of the age continuum (young people who are deemed to have no experience or insight and older people who are assumed either to have 'disengaged' from active life, or to no longer possess the faculties necessary for analytical thinking) do not need to be active partners in decision-making processes. As a result they are often left out of debates such as how scarce resources should be spent, who a young person should live with, whether independent living is in someone's best interests and so on. Ignoring or 'sidelining' either group on such grounds constitutes ageist practice, so how can we guard against this? One potentially empowering strategy is that of user involvement.

What is user involvement? This term has been around in the social care field for a number of decades now and it is fair to say that there has been a significant rise in the number of users of services who are either insisting on having a say in decisions affecting their welfare and life-chances, or responding to invitations to contribute to the decision-making processes that go on in government departments, hospitals, schools, local authorities and so on. Indeed, participation by service users is something that has been actively promoted by the government through legislation and policy directives. For example, as I write, the Welsh Assembly is looking to establish a National Partnership Forum for Older People and there are moves to ensure that all young people in Britain have representation in the form of Children's Commissioners.

A strong case for a shift in the balance of power in terms of decision making has been made by people with physical and learning disabilities and users of mental health services in particular, who have long argued that their expertise in their own situation merits being considered alongside that of professionals, policy makers and financing bodies. For example, Strong (2003) suggests that, while issues about their mental health are cross-cut by other aspects such as gender, ethnic background and so on, user groups have enough in common to constitute a national movement – an indication of how far the agenda for change has moved. Similarly, progress in terms of challenging the assumption that people with learning disabilities do not have the capacity to contribute to decision-making is evident in the success of organisations such as People First. The involvement of older people and children has been a little slower to get off the mark, but is, nevertheless, gathering momentum over recent years. You might want to consider the part ageist ideology may have played in explaining these disparities within the overall movement?

User involvement is a very broad term and there is a danger that it can be addressed in a tokenistic way. Hickey (1994) analyses user involvement in terms of a 'participation continuum', which ranges from a situation in which service users are merely informed of decisions already taken to one in which they are able to exercise control for themselves.

Exercise 2.3

What avenues for making your views known have been open to you during:

    (a) your childhood?

    (b) your adolescence?

    (c) your adulthood?

Were these processes effective? If not, what would have made you feel more valued or empowered?

Before moving on to think about how we can promote good practice in this field, we might think about its benefits.

What can user involvement achieve? While there may be specific aims and objectives for individual cases, at a broader level involving service users can serve to give out the message that people have a right to a say in decision making which affects their lives. This, in itself, can help to challenge the tendency for some people to internalise the ageist messages around them – those that tell them they 'don't know their own minds' or are 'past it'. As we have seen, children and young people are not always listened to adequately, even in situations which affect them and their life chances in a big way. The Children Act 1989 attempted to give them a voice but it is not always the case that this voice is heard in situations where the process is managed by adults with concerns and agendas of their own. In a newspaper article about how public bodies are responding to the call to listen to children, Inman (2003) makes reference to the danger of tokenism if only those who come forward to consulting bodies are consulted and the views of 'hard to reach' young people are not actively sought.

It can provide an opportunity for politicisation and what Freire (1972) refers to as 'conscientisation'. That is, it raises an awareness in people of what is happening around them and reminds them that they do not have to just sit back and take what is thrown at them. But raising awareness and inviting participation are not enough if that participation is not facilitated.

How can it be put into practice? A good starting point is to ask people how they would like to be involved and what level of participation they feel comfortable with. Some people feel threatened by the thought of taking part in a public meeting or discussion forum but might be perfectly happy to get involved as an observer, or feed their opinions into the process via an advocate. Others may be keen to be involved at the level of local politics but may be prevented from doing so by difficulties such as actually getting to meetings and following the agenda and pace once they get there. For example, some older people have problems with sitting for long stretches at a time, or with reading presentations on overhead projectors or screens. Where the agenda is pre-set by one party then the other can be put at a disadvantage, especially when discussions are couched in jargonistic terminology or make reference to concepts which may be unfamiliar to some. As we have seen, many older people are also carers for dependent relatives and may be disadvantaged unless their needs as carers are recognised and responded to, such as with the provision of respite facilities for those dependent on them. Where children and young people are involved, it may be necessary to work with schools and colleges, to ensure that involvement is facilitated in a way which does not disadvantage them. Inclusion can also be hampered if organisers assume that all participants can speak and understand the language they intend to present in, as too can neglecting to make arrangements that allow people who have visual or hearing impairments to participate.

Attendance at meetings is not the only way in which older and younger service users can have their say. The following are but a few examples of other options and you will probably be able to think of more:

- the use of questionnaires to elicit research evidence;
- employing advocates to boost confidence and self-esteem, thereby encouraging participation;

- outreach initiatives which arrange for consultations to take place in people's own homes, rather than expecting them to attend group consultations elsewhere: and,
- the facilitating of service user participation in training and inspection work.

The possibilities are too diverse to offer advice about in a book such as this and the practicalities are something for individual organisations to apply themselves to. What is important is taking on board the principle that it is unfair to continue with practices which exclude people from democratic participation, or contribute to the message that their participation is not important. As I have argued elsewhere (Thompson, 1997) of older people and social workers:

> If user involvement is offered to older users in a tokenistic way, allowing them access to only the bottom rungs of the participation ladder . . . then it appears to be being interpreted by service providers in a way that preserves the power imbalance between user and social worker, rather than challenges it. A reinterpretation of the term involvement, which allows access to the higher rungs of the participation ladder, those of joint decision-making and control, depends on users being seen as worthy of it. (p. 40)

Of course, this discussion is not just about social work, but can be applied to any form of people work. Anti-ageist practice asks that we evaluate whether, in whatever field of work we are involved, we treat people differently and less inclusively on the grounds of assumptions about age. Unless there is a system whereby service user feedback can be sought, considered and acted upon, then any evaluation of services will be missing a vitally important component. There has been a considerable amount of progress of late in terms of service user involvement but it has to be one which values the opinions of all, not just those who can make their voices heard easily, or who recognise their right to be heard.

Practice Focus 2.4

The Community Centre had been lucky enough to receive a significant amount of money, bequeathed to them by a local benefactor. The management committee decided to use it to put some ideas they had been discussing into practice and the centre was closed temporarily for refurbishment. When it re-opened the local community was thrilled to find that computers and Internet facilities had been installed. Not only that but a set of side rooms had been furnished and accessorised to function as a 'reminiscence suite', so that people could be reminded of the sights, sounds and smells of years gone by.

The opening day celebrations were held one afternoon in the school holidays so that the young people who used the centre as a youth club in the evenings could attend alongside the senior citizens group. Everyone was impressed and there was a buzz of excitement and optimism about the new facilities. However, it wasn't long before the excitement turned to disappointment. Several of the young people were fascinated by the reminiscence suite and were keen to learn more about their history and that of the local area, but found that it was to be open only one afternoon each week, when they would be in school. Similarly, a significant number of the older people wanted to take advantage of the IT facilities and had hoped that their afternoon club could be developed into an Internet cafe. When they discovered that their use was to be supervised by a youth development worker, and only during the youth club sessions, they too were disappointed.

It became quite clear that those planning the changes, while trying to respond to the needs of the different age groups, had actually used age as a criterion for exclusion. In doing so, they had not only been influenced by stereotypical assumptions but had also lost out on an opportunity to promote intergenerational-ity. That is, they could have helped break down barriers between different age cohorts and shown others in the community that each group could enhance the learning of the other.

Vulnerability: a self-fulfilling prophecy?

We have seen that ageist ideology works to portray those at each extreme of the age spectrum as vulnerable and ineffectual. It fuels the stereotype and that image makes it appear legitimate to push people to the margins of society. But it is worth giving some thought to whether we play a part in the process of creating that vulnerability in the first place That is to say, do we *make* certain people vulnerable and then blame them for *becoming* vulnerable? For example, do we place older people and children in situations where they are more likely to become victims of abuse, and then consider them as vulnerable people because that abuse occurs? Does the way in which the economy is run make it likely that a significant number of children and older people will live in poverty, and then conceptualise them as vulnerable because they cannot protect themselves from theft, cold weather and so on. Brown (2002) uses such examples to illustrate what she refers to as a 'social model of vulnerability', which is the idea that vulnerability can be created by social factors such as the way systems are organised, rather than being totally attributable to psychological attributes such as coping skills. In the following quotation, she highlights systems of care delivery as an example of the social approach to explaining vulnerability:

> Arguably, there are particular or additional risks arising out of the abnormal situations in which they are placed. Many older or disabled service users, for example, are more exposed to risk than others because more people have intimate access to them in their daily lives. There may be different home carers coming into their private space every day, perhaps someone they don't know coming in to wash, bathe or dress them. They may find themselves travelling to hospital with a volunteer they have not

met before. Many people would feel vulnerable in these sorts of situations. In other words, the vulnerability of those who use care services may be compounded by the way their care needs are met. (p. 22)

Taking this approach on board should lead us to question whether practices do, indeed, create or compound vulnerability. This is something which only you or your organisation can evaluate properly, but the following questions should provide a starting point for that process:

- Are employees and volunteers given training and advice to equip them for the jobs they do, or are they expected to rely on their own judgement, which may be uninformed or at odds with the organisation? Are you putting people at risk because of this?
- Are rights issues high on your organisation's agenda?
- Does your organisation value the opinions of everyone, regardless of age, and put this into practice by having effective communication channels so that people don't feel powerless or excluded?

On a broader level, you might want to consider the following issues:

- Do we fail to ask children and young people their opinion on matters of importance to them and them blame them when they react in a negative way to decisions made by others? For example, consider a family deciding to take a holiday without consulting the children about location and then having considerable dissatisfaction and tension when they do not feel happy there.
- Do we, as a society, create conditions of poverty which make it difficult for older people to participate in matters such as politics and education, and then blame them for not participating when they cannot afford the necessary transport and subsistence costs to do so?

Again, in an introductory book such as this, it is only possible to skim over the surface of such complex issues. My intention in highlighting a social model of vulnerability has been merely to provide further food for thought on the subject of ageism. If we accept the argument that vulnerability is not necessarily an inherent part of being old or young, but can be socially constructed, then this opens up the possibility of our being able to play some part in challenging it.

Conclusion

These have been just a few examples of many that could have been drawn on to underline how age discrimination occurs, often unnoticed, and to provide food for thought about how it can be brought out into the open and addressed. Because of space constraints a lot has remained unsaid, but I hope you will now feel inspired to read further around these ideas and issues and to debate them with managers, colleagues and those who use your services. Despite the best efforts of activists within youth movements and organisations such as Pensioners' Voice, change may be hampered by the internalisation of ideas that some people are less worthy of rights and respect than others. Reflecting on your own values and practice, and raising awareness of age discrimination in others, can play a very significant part in the anti-ageist challenge, but an emphasis on challenging age discrimination should not blind us to the other forms of discrimination that exist alongside it. I have argued that age is an important aspect of our identity and one that is often used as a justification for unfair allocation of resources and respect, but so too are gender, ethnicity, religion, sexual orientation and so on. In Part Three we will move the discussion on to consider how ageism does not operate independently of other forms of oppression, but rather interacts with them.

Part Three: Discrimination and Oppression

Introduction

In the preceding two parts of the book the emphasis has been on exploring the ways in which discrimination on the grounds of age contributes to a situation in which older people, children and adolescents can be marginalised and disempowered. However, as we have already seen, it is not something which operates in isolation from other experiences. Our age is part of who we are, but so too are any number of other aspects, such as our ethnicity, class, gender and so on – and any or all of these can serve as a basis for people being treated less favourably than others around us.

That is not to say that we are not important as individual beings. Psychological and biological studies have much to contribute to our understanding of growing and ageing but, in order to better understand age discrimination, we need to consider not just the individual, but also the social and cultural contexts in which we live our lives and the external structures and processes which help to shape our life experiences and life chances. In doing so it will become clear that we cannot separate ageism out completely from other forms of discrimination, and must take on board that many people experience what is often referred to as 'multiple oppressions'. For example, those who have been marginalised throughout their lives because of their class position may have this situation made worse by being further marginalised on the grounds of age, when they reach their latter years. Gay people who have experienced oppression throughout their lives because of their sexuality may find that this not only continues into their old age, but actually gets worse in old age because of ageist ideology's tendency to deny older people a sexual identity at all (these are points to which I will return below).

What we need to consider, then, is not only the psychology of the individual, but also the sociological factors that have such an important bearing on shaping the experiences of older people at one end of the age spectrum, and children and young people at the other. The discipline of sociology highlights how societies are divided along particular recognisable lines. Drawing on geological terminology, reference is often made to societies being 'stratified' along 'fault lines' which include such aspects as ethnicity, class, gender, religion, sexual orientation, physical and intellectual ability and so on. In this way we can see that society is characterised by 'social divisions' – structured patterns that divide one group of people from others. For example, the social division of gender divides people into the categories of men and women and assigns different expectations in relation to behaviour (masculine behaviour versus feminine behaviour), work patterns (the 'sexual division of labour', as sociologists call it), life chances and so on. Older people and children are affected by these social divisions, just as any other age group are. It is therefore important to consider the significance of social divisions for those people who face discrimination on the grounds of age.

In the discussion that follows we will consider how these social divisions, and the processes associated with them, serve to exacerbate the effects of age discrimination but, before doing so, we will look in a little more detail at the significance of ageism as a form of discrimination in its own right.

Exercise 3.1

Write down how you would describe yourself in terms of class position. Once you have done this, write down three ways in which you think this has made a difference to your life.

Now repeat the process with some of the other forms of social division that locate you in society, such as:

- your gender;
- your ethnicity;
- whether you are disabled or able-bodied;
- your sexual orientation;
- your religion; and
- your age.

What does this tell you about the importance of social structures?

Ageism

Anti-discriminatory practice in general has been on the agenda of the helping professions for quite some time now, but it is only relatively recently that the concept of ageism as a significant form of discrimination has become established as an area of concern, and the anti-ageist movement, while gaining in influence, is still a relatively new one. The role of age as a basis for unfair discrimination has a long way to go before its significance achieves anything even vaguely approaching the attention given to racism and sexism. And, even where attention is paid to ageism, it tends to focus predominantly on issues relating to old age without considering how age discrimination can also apply in major ways to children and young people and, indeed, at any stage in the life course.

This is not to suggest that there should be a competition for attention amongst different forms of discrimination (the 'hierarchy of oppressions' as it is sometimes known – Thompson, 2001), but rather to argue that an adequate understanding of discrimination needs to be broad based, rather than narrowly focused. Forms of discrimination are not separate, unconnected entities, but rather different dimensions of people's experience. I shall return to this point below.

For anti-ageist policies and practices to be taken seriously in their own right, they have to be given the profile they deserve. They have to be seen as important matters in themselves and not simply as an 'add on' to concerns about more well-established forms of discrimination. As we saw in Part Two, ageism affects large numbers of people and is therefore not a minor or peripheral concern. It can be seen as a serious social problem.

As we have seen, in the current climate attempts to challenge discrimination and its consequences are often trivialised by being conceptualised as a 'fad' rather than a genuine commitment to promoting high-quality practice when working with older people, children and teenagers. Thompson (1996) argues that, rather than just being the latest in a long line of anti-discriminatory 'causes', the anti-ageist challenge has a moral dimension that is undermined by those who misrepresent it as fussing unnecessarily over the use of terminology:

> The empowerment of older people as a strategy of anti-ageist practice must be seen as a moral imperative – an essential part of a principled approach to the care of older people – for . . . good practice must be anti-discriminatory practice. To avoid issues of discrimination or to deal with them at the superficial level of a fad or fashion, is to condone the oppression such discrimination engenders. On such important matters there can be no morally neutral ground – to fail to tackle ageism is to subscribe to its continuation, to allow it to flourish unchallenged. (p. 33)

The tendency to portray discriminatory process as just a procession of 'isms,' each coming to prominence in its own 'fashionable' era, detracts from the point that these do not operate in a conceptual or theoretical vacuum, but rather relate to real people and real life experiences. The people who experience ageing and ageism do not do so as *just* older people or *just* children and young people, but as multifaceted individuals – a disabled white man, a black child of working-class parents, a woman with mental health problems, a homeless young Irish man, a lesbian woman with a learning disability, and so on. Given that the experience of many people is one of multiple oppressions, the remainder of Part Three will move on from this discussion of ageism as a form of oppression in its own right to a consideration of how it interacts with other forms of oppression.

Ageism and sexism

The Women's Movement has played a significant part in ensuring that, at the beginning of the 21st century, we have a much greater awareness of the importance of gender in shaping social life and personal identity than was the case at the beginning of the 20th century. Although many people still adopt what is known as a 'gender-blind' approach (that is, one which fails to recognise or address the significance of gender as an influence in people's lives and as a factor in determining the distribution of power and life chances), on the whole gender features much more as part of our thinking about individuals and groups. However, despite this greater level of awareness of gender, there still remains a significant gap when it comes to exploring how issues of gender and age inter-relate. We still have a long way to go before we have an adequate understanding of how these two social divisions combine to play such an important role in people's experiences. We can, none the less, consider at least some of the linkages between the two.

The relationship between ageism and sexism can be appreciated when one considers that, in more advanced old age at least, the majority of older people are women. This can be seen in the following figures taken from the United Kingdom 2001 census:

Age Range	Males	Females
60–64	1,409,676	1,470,272
70–74	1,059,151	1,280,080
80–84	482,697	830,850
90 and over	83,202	288,067

(Source: National Statistics Website – www.statistics.gov.uk)

There is ample evidence to suggest that, rather than having been eradicated by the equal opportunities agenda, discrimination on the grounds of gender is still a major feature of women's lives (see, for example, Ledwith and Colgan, 1996). Furthermore, authors such as Hughes and Mtezuka (1992) and Bernard and Meade (1993) have argued that it is still a feature of women's lives in *old* age, and they highlight a tendency for the particular experiences of older women to attract less interest and recognition than those of their younger counterparts, so that the fight for women's rights does not recognise women once they have become defined under the category of 'aged'. There is not sufficient space in this book to debate the history of the feminist challenge in general, although you will find suggested reading in Part Four if you want to develop your understanding in that area. It is enough for our purposes here to take on board that, for women in old age, the discrimination they experience because of their age cannot be divorced from the discrimination they continue to experience because of their gender – the two feed into, and act as props for, each other:

> Gender and ageing are inextricably intertwined in social life; each can only be fully understood with reference to the other. As we age, we are influenced by the societal, cultural, economic and political context prevailing at different times in our life course. Thus the connectedness of gender and ageing stems both from social change over time and from age-related life course events; social history and personal biography are interwoven over time. (Ginn and Arber, 1995, p. 1)

If we think back to the theory base discussed in Part One we can identify that these processes can operate at different levels. Consider, for example, the forces which operate at the cultural level to put pressure on both men and women to conform to stereotypical gender roles. Despite their increased participation in the labour market, it is still the norm for child-rearing and domestic work around the home to be seen largely as the responsibility of women, and providing for and protecting the family to be considered to be the most appropriate role for men. The power of ideology which promotes these arrangements as 'right and proper' is such that it is a role or set of roles that many men and women come to accept as something they either do, or feel they *should* do. This is perhaps especially true of the present cohort of women in their 70s and 80s, who would have been influenced by post-war propaganda to provide the domestic support necessary to rebuild the new and harmonious society envisaged after the turmoil of the Second World War.

The development of feminist thinking has highlighted how women have been oppressed by the pressure to conform to typical roles and codes of behaviour and expect to be treated in different and less favourable ways, purely on the grounds of gender – consider, for example, the issue of equal pay, with women still earning significantly less than men. The New Earnings Survey (National Statistics Website) indicates that, in 2003, female full-time workers receive only 82 per cent of the hourly rate that male workers receive. But what happens when women reach old age? The experience of many is that the roles for which they have been valued throughout their younger days are no longer significant and so the status they provided is lost to them. Consider the following examples:

- the capacity to bear children;
- being a home maker, especially if they move into group living situations; and
- caring for others.

Practice Focus 3.1

Mrs Chandra had moved into Elm Villas, a retirement complex, some months ago. She had realised that her chronic ill health was making it difficult for her to continue to manage the running of the house that had been her pride and joy for so many years. Even after her husband had died and her daughter had moved to live with a friend, she insisted on making sure that she cleaned all the rooms regularly and kept them in good order. The rest of her family thought her efforts were a waste of time and the effort damaging to her health, and put pressure on her to move into Elm Villas where she could enjoy a well-earned rest and leave the domestic arrangements for someone else to worry about. After much persuasion, and with a lot of apprehension, Mrs Chandra agreed to move there. But after several months, her family were concerned that, far from looking rested, she looked more haggard and seemed to be withdrawn but put it down to her frustration at growing old and being in poor health. She hadn't taken up any of the social invitations offered to her and had not made any new friendships. She looked so unhappy that her niece took her to one side and asked her whether she regretted the decision she had taken to sell her house. She was taken aback to hear that Mrs Chandra was not missing the house itself but was missing her role in keeping it running as a household – even though she had lived there alone. When she explained that keeping house was what she felt good at, and what people had admired her for all of her adult life, her niece began to understand. Mrs Chandra had lost the role which had given her a purpose and status in life and she had so fully taken on the role that society had shaped for her that she felt worthless and guilty when she was relieved of it. Her niece now began to see the wider picture and could see how the family had neglected to consider how the pressures Mrs Chandra had felt as a woman throughout her life continued to be significant in her old age.

When considering how ageism interacts with sexism we must not forget that it is not just women who are adversely affected by stereotypical assumptions about gender roles, but men too. Expectations of men as providers and protectors can also lead to loss of role and status on retirement from the world of work and in situations where they experience declining health or strength. As with all such debates, this is obviously not always the case. Indeed, Friedan (1993), in her interviews with older Americans, cites a fairly commonly held view of old age as a time of life which is open to redefinition and where there is a sense of 'no longer being bound by the old restrictions of masculine versus feminine competition' (p. 132). Many would argue, though, that these 'restrictions' continue to impact on older people's lives and add to the disadvantage they already experience on the grounds of their age alone. For example, Rose and Bruce (1995) observe that older men are often accorded higher status as carers than are their female counterparts because gender stereotyping suggests that this is not a typically ascribed role for men or one for which they are well equipped. Where older women act as carers it is not considered to be something which should attract any particular praise, whereas older men are likely to attract not only praise, but also extra status and assistance:

caring is seen as normal and natural to women, but something special when performed by men. The superior gender brings esteem to a task undervalued when done by women – particularly older women . . . Their [men's] advantage seemed to be that merely to attempt to care is admirable in a man, whereas for a woman it is her natural duty, and not only should she attempt it, but she feels under an obligation to perform well. The differential esteem felt by and for the older carer speaks eloquently of the long and deforming fingers of gender. (p. 128)

Gender is, of course, a very significant part of growing up, as it is through the process of socialisation that we learn gender roles and form an attachment to particular patterns of thought, feelings and actions. It would be naïve, therefore, to fail to take account of gender as a factor that intersects with age to shape the lives of children and young people. Consider the following range of issues:

- *Education:* Children's experiences of the education system reveal significant gender differences – for example, the bias towards physical sciences and maths for boys and arts subjects and languages for girls (Wilson, 2003). These 'gendered' influences are likely to have a major impact in terms of shaping future life chances and even on the individual's sense of self or identity (Cranny-Francis *et al.*, 2003).
- *Crime:* Offending patterns amongst children and young people also show distinct gender patterns (Coles and Maile, 2002). This refers to not only the extent of criminal activity but also the type. Clearly such matters can have a major bearing on future life experiences.
- *The sexual division of labour:* Gender-influenced patterns of occupation choice tend to appear at a relatively early age. As Connell (2002) comments of socialisation and schools in particular:

> Institutions do not mechanically determine young people's learning. But they do shape the consequences of what young people do – the risks they run, the recognition they get, the networks they gain access to, the penalties they pay. For instance, adopting a particular pattern of masculinity may strongly affect the academic success a boy experiences in school, and thus the occupational paths open to him later. (p. 80)

This 'division of labour' along gender lines applies to not only paid work in the public sphere but also unpaid work in the private sphere – that is, housework.

What these points illustrate is the subtle but important interrelationship between gender as a social division and age – which also acts as a social division, in the sense that it divides people into socially significant groups according to their age. Age is socially significant, especially when it intersects with gender.

What this means is that, while an individual's gender is hugely significant in terms of shaping life experiences, how that gender is experienced and how it shapes our lives, varies according to our age. Gender influences and age influences flow together to have a powerful effect on our thoughts, feelings, actions and relationships.

While 'sex' (male or female) is a biological category, 'gender' is socially constructed – that is, what constitutes 'masculine' or 'feminine' behaviour is socially defined (as is illustrated by the fact that notions of masculinity and femininity vary from culture to culture and society to society (horizontal variation) and over time or through history (vertical variation) – consider, for example, Henry VIII's dress, which was considered very masculine at the time.

Gender, then, is something we 'do' rather than something we 'have'. This being the case, one thing we can recognise is that there is a very strong tendency for us to 'do' gender differently at different ages. For example, crying in public may be seen as 'normal' for a small boy, but is likely to be perceived differently in a grown man.

Exercise 3.2

Make a list of five to ten characteristics that you feel are different according to gender. Consider such issues as dress, work roles, emotional responses and so on.

Once you have established your list, consider each one carefully in terms of whether you feel age makes a difference. For example, can you identify any ways in which a distinction applies between younger men and women but which tends to disappear or at least feature less in old age?

Clearly, then, the way a person lives their life in terms of gender will be influenced to a certain extent at least by age. Similarly, how a person experiences moving from one stage of the life course to another will owe much to their gender and the social implications of being assigned characteristics of masculinity and femininity.

Ageism and class

Socioeconomic position or 'class' has long been recognised as a major influence on people's lives. A person's class position can change over time – in either direction – and can therefore be different at different ages as we move through the life course. However, even where a person's class position remains stable, age can still be a major factor. This is because, just as age and gender issues intersect, so too do issues relating to age and class. This applies to both ends of the age spectrum. We shall begin by considering old age and class before looking at how class issues inter-relate with issues connected with childhood and adolescence.

As long ago as 1982, Chris Phillipson, an important commentator on issues relating to old age, pointed out that there is a significant relationship between class and age. He argued convincingly that old age has the effect of amplifying poverty. That is, if someone has experienced low levels of income throughout their lives, the onset of old age is likely to make the situation worse, perhaps plunging them into poverty. For others, even where they have enjoyed a relatively good standard of living in their lives, they may find themselves in financial difficulties if they have not made adequate pension provision.

Although financial position is clearly an important part of class as a social division, it is not the only one. Other important factors include, for example, lifestyle issues. If someone has invested a great deal of money in leisure goods such as sports or gardening equipment, for example, then they are likely to be able to benefit from that investment after retirement. However, for people who have not had the disposable income to make such an investment, they will not have such leisure resources to fall back on and are unlikely to be able to make the investment required once they have retired. Such matters can therefore have the effect of widening social inequalities in old age.

It is important to remember that old age is not simply 'death's waiting room'. Such a stereotypical view is a gross distortion of reality. Many people who would today be labelled as 'elderly' may be 25 years or longer away from death. The ageist assumption that older people are 'at death's door' is both inaccurate and unhelpful. When we talk about poverty in old age, then, we should recognise that we are talking about what could well be a major proportion of an individual's life.

At the other end of the age spectrum, there is now a wealth of research evidence to show that significant numbers of children live in poverty. For example, a study in Northern Ireland found that more than a third of children live below the poverty line (Hillyard *et al.*, 2003). Another study, undertaken on a broader scale across 46 countries, found that more than a billion children are suffering poverty (UNICEF, 2003). Child poverty is clearly a widespread problem – a fact which emphasises how important it is to recognise the interplay of factors associated with class and age.

Poverty is a particularly significant issue in relation to age for, as Thompson (1995) points out:

> poverty can exacerbate and complicate other problems. For example, poverty can lead to tensions that trigger aggression or feelings of helplessness that underpin depression. Poverty can therefore be seen as not only a problem in its own right, but also a significant dimension of a range of other problems. (p. 76)

Clearly, then, issues of poverty and deprivation, and of socioeconomic class more broadly, have a very important bearing on matters relating to age. If we wish to develop an adequate understanding of age discrimination, we must also take account of class and its effects on people's lives at various stages in the life course.

Ageism and racism

Just as oppression on the grounds of gender is not something that one leaves behind on reaching old age, nor is the potential for racism to impact on one's quality of life. The point has already been made that age is one of the factors that contributes to quality of life issues, particularly given, as we have just noted above, the links between age and poverty at both ends of the age spectrum. So too is race, or perhaps more accurately, the broader concept of ethnicity which incorporates not just skin colour and other physical characteristics, but also a number of other aspects which make us feel a belonging to a particular group or community, as this excerpt from a definition by Storkey (1991) indicates: 'all the characteristics which go up to make cultural identity; origins, physical appearance, language, family structure, religious beliefs, politics' (pp. 109–10).

Exercise 3.3

Think about your own identity. What is it about you that makes you the unique person that you are? Think about a situation in which you have been treated as 'just another face in the crowd' – perhaps when complaining to a large company or something similar. How did that make you feel? Can you see parallels with ageism?

A commonly used term in the literature is 'double jeopardy' – the idea that age and race combine to be doubly oppressive for black elders. Given the evidence which suggests that those from ethnic minorities are over-represented in the poverty statistics (Pilkington, 2003, Solomos, 2003), as are older people (Marshall and Rowlings, 1998), it is not hard to see how being old and being a member of an ethnic minority can be particularly disadvantaging. Indeed, the National Service Framework (Department of Health, 2001) has taken this on board in its policy directives. This reference to the combination of class, age and race factors has been referred to as 'triple jeopardy'. It is a term commonly associated with the work of Alison Norman who defined it as people being: 'at risk because they are old, because of the physical conditions and hostility under which they have to live, and because services are not accessible to them' (1985, p. 1). However, Blakemore and Boneham (1994) point out that this definition mixes up causes of disadvantage (age, race and hostility, for example) with the effects or outcomes of such disadvantage (lack of access to services). None the less, this remains an important concept and Norman's work has made an important contribution to raising awareness of the interaction of different social divisions to produce oppressive outcomes.

One important thing that racism and ageism have in common is an emphasis on dehumanisation – lumping people together in broad categories, rather than recognising each individual as a unique person in their own right. Differences of language, religion, life view, dress and so on can all be incorporated within one label – for example, Asian. We therefore have to be very careful to make sure that we are not falling into the trap of dehumanising people by seeing them simply as members of a category ('the elderly' or 'black people') and losing sight of the fact that their age, their ethnicity and so on, are dimensions of who they are, but an individual is always more than the sum of their parts. The double disadvantage of ageism and racism can intensify the tendency towards dehumanisation, and so we need to be wary of the danger of being carried along by such a powerful tendency.

Of course, it is not only older people who can be seen to be doubly disadvantaged, as ageism in relation to children and young people also intersects with racism. This can be seen to apply in such areas of particular disadvantage as:

- *Education:* educational success (or otherwise) can be seen to follow racial lines. For example, Owusu-Bempah, (2001) cites evidence which suggests that children from ethnic minority groups are treated less favourably than other children, mentioning processes such as exclusion and harassment. German (1996) captures the point well when he argues that:

  > As far as black people in Britain are concerned, one of the biggest obstacles to their children's success and security is racism. What they would like to see is teachers and schools availing themselves of every opportunity to eradicate the effects of racist attitudes and practices in all aspects of school life so that they can enjoy their full share of equality with regard to educational access, treatment and outcome. (p. 61)

- *Health care:* Ethnic group differences in both morbidity (experiences of ill health) and mortality (life expectancy) have been well documented (Dyson and Smaje, 2001). Such differences can also be found amongst children and young people. Ill health can be a major problem at any time in life, but the particular significance of illness experienced during childhood and adolescence can be immense in terms of its influence in shaping a child or young person's outlook on life.

- *Child protection:* Sadly we can even find evidence of racism in the child protection system. Channer and Parton (1990) comment on how cultural relativism, that is the assumption that no one culture should claim moral superiority over any other, can lead to black children being disadvantaged:

  > The notion of 'cultural relativism' articulates the view that white social workers have particular problems in assessing minimum childcare standards when working with families that do not conform to their own views about family life. However, rather than over-react as they may previously have done by admitting large numbers of black children to care, the implication is that they hesitate to intervene at all and hence put children from black families in real and serious danger. (p. 111)

It is worrying to think that black children can be afforded less protection because of the role of institutional racism in influencing the effectiveness or otherwise of child protection measures.

Practice Focus 3.2

Ayesha was 10 years old when she moved to live in a children's residential unit, when her family situation broke down. Even before she arrived she had been allocated a keyworker, Nadia, who worked hard to make the transition as easy as possible for Ayesha. Not wanting to fall into the trap of treating her as 'just another child' she gathered as much information as she could about her home and school life, so that she could prepare a care plan that would be individualised and would meet Ayesha's specific needs.

She fully expected Ayesha to take a while to settle into her new surroundings and to feel confident enough to make friends at the unit and at school. However, after a month or two it became clear to Nadia that Ayesha was becoming increasingly unhappy and withdrawn. She did not want to go to school and preferred to stay in her room even when there were opportunities to go out shopping or to the youth club in the town. Nadia looked to guidance from colleagues but could not identify what the problem was until Ayesha was visited by an older cousin who expressed dismay at how dry Ayesha's skin was and how unkempt her hair had become. That evening the cousin returned with some of the skin and hair care products that Ayesha was used to and set about oiling her skin and styling her hair quite differently. Nadia felt a bit affronted that the attention she had paid to Ayesha's personal care had been criticised. After all, she had encouraged her to wash and brush her hair every day, which is how she looked after her own hair. What she came to realise was that she had not attended to the specific needs of Ayesha as a child from a particular culture, nor recognised the importance that was attached to looking well groomed.

When Nadia next worked with Ayesha she talked to her about these matters and Ayesha explained how having her hair and skin oiled had been a familiar ritual for her for as long as she could remember, and that she hadn't felt good about her appearance since coming to live in the unit. When reflecting on matters afterwards Nadia came to realise that her approach had been discriminatory in more than one respect. Not only had she denied Ayesha the chance to contribute to her own care plan on the grounds of her age, but also her ethnocentric view had resulted in Ayesha's needs not being met in some respects. That is, she had looked at things from within her own cultural perspective and worked on the assumption that her way was the 'right' way to do things.

Ageism, heterosexism and sexual identity

Sexuality in relation to children has long been seen as a taboo area – and understandably so, given the dangers of sexual abuse that exist in modern society. However, what is perhaps not appreciated to the same extent is that sexuality in old age can also be seen as a 'no go' area. Indeed, the idea of older people having a sex life is often the subject of ridicule, as if sexuality in old age were in some way 'inappropriate' (Gibson, 1992; Thompson, 1995; Davies,

2001). We may find ourselves laughing at such matters without actually realising the implications of denying (or stigmatising) a connection between sexual desire and old age. The relationship between age and sexuality is clearly a very complex one, and prone to considerable oversimplification.

Bevan and Thompson (2003) make an important comment on sexual identity when they argue that:

> sexuality is an intrinsic component of being human: it is bound together in our identity and sense of well-being. The sexual dimension of being human is therefore inextricably related to our physical, emotional, psychological, spiritual and social selves as individual beings. (p. 186)

To deny someone such an important aspect of their identity is clearly oppressive. To do so simply because a person has reached a certain age is perhaps doubly so.

For a person's sexual identity to be denied or stigmatised at any age can be a source of oppression, but where this occurs in conjunction with the discrimination people experience on the grounds of age (mainly, but not exclusively, at either end of the age spectrum), the situation can be seen as potentially very damaging. I shall explore these issues as they relate to both older people and children and young people, beginning with a consideration of gay and lesbian relationships in old age.

When we consider that same sex relationships still generate a great deal of disapproval in many quarters, we can begin to appreciate how difficult and complex issues about same sex relationships in old age can be. An important concept in this regard is 'heterosexism'. This refers to a form of discrimination premised on the assumption that homosexuality is 'abnormal' or 'pathological' – terms which suggest that there is a dominant view about sexuality and sexual relationships which serves to disadvantage those who do not fit *naturally* with the norm. Wise (2000) explains this in the following passage:

> everyone is assumed to be heterosexual unless proven otherwise, and anyone not fitting into this pattern is considered to be abnormal, sick, morally corrupt and inferior . . . Just as the concepts of racism and sexism have helped us to understand the oppression of black people and women, so the concept of heterosexism has assisted us in theorising lesbian and gay oppression. (p. 154)

While heterosexism can be seen as a significant form of oppression at any age, we can note that it takes on an extra dimension for those who are both homosexual and at one end of the age spectrum or the other. This raises important implications for how we work with older people. For example, we should be very careful not to fall into the trap of assuming that an elderly person is heterosexual (or, worse still, that they are asexual).

Sexuality, as we have noted, is an important part of a person's identity, and so to make potentially discriminatory assumptions can be a major problem and is therefore very much to be avoided.

There is also a gender dimension to these issues. This is because sexuality has traditionally been defined in male terms (consider, for example, how sexuality tends to be portrayed in the media). This means that female sexuality has tended to receive less attention. According to a report by Vincent *et al.* (2000), there is a lack of knowledge about how women define sexuality as they age. We therefore still have a great deal to learn about sexual identity in old age.

Practice Focus 3.3

Tony had been diagnosed with his illness several years ago, when he was in his early 70s. He knew only too well that his condition was incurable and that he would continue to deteriorate to the extent that, before long, he would be totally dependent on others for every aspect of his physical care. Already he felt bad about relying on Jack, his life partner for more than 25 years, and had come to the decision that the quality of their relationship would be enhanced if he moved to a residential setting where there would be paid carers on hand all of the time. Jack was not at all keen on the idea at first, but felt better after reading the 'Statement of Values' in the home's promotional literature and the reassurance given by the manager that Tony would be treated as a person with his own unique needs.

However, this commitment did not appear to be borne out in practice. Both Tony and Jack had found the transition very traumatic and wanted to spend as much time together as they could. They had always been very demonstrative in their love for each other and found hugging and physical intimacy comforting. Jack would spend at least part of every day with Tony in his room and often lay beside him on the bed and embraced him, as had been their usual practice when either of them had felt ill or anxious. While there had been no overt disapproval of their displays of intimacy, they were both very aware of the embarrassed looks on the faces of carers when they entered the room, and they had overheard discussions about how 'weird' it was for people 'of their age' to be behaving in such a manner. And, although they had expected a more enlightened attitude from people working in the caring professions, they were only too aware that it was intimacy between two men, as well as intimacy between two older people, that was providing a talking point among the staff.

They had hoped that, as Tony's condition deteriorated, it would be possible for Jack to sleep with him, as those long hours were the time when they both needed the reassurance that physical closeness brought. From their experience so far, they began to doubt whether this would be possible, or even desirable, given the atmosphere it was likely to promote. So much for 'unique needs', thought Jack. After all, they weren't asking for much, surely? Just that they be allowed to comfort each other without being judged according to heterosexist and ageist perceptions of what is 'appropriate'.

The situation relating to sexuality for children and young people is also a very complex area. On the one hand we have to recognise that sexuality is not something that begins in adulthood or even adolescence – it would be a mistake to deny elements of sexuality in childhood – while, on the other, we need to acknowledge the very real and very important issue of the sexual abuse of children.

The Children Act 1989 provides a framework for dealing with these issues (in England and Wales) in so far as it both addresses the need for sexual identity (including same sex relationships) to be taken into consideration in working with young people and provides for their protection from sexual abuse. Of course, the law does not guarantee that such matters will be appropriately handled but it does at least give us a framework from which to operate.

Sexual abuse has been defined as:

> forcing or enticing a child or young person to take part in sexual activities, whether or not the child is aware of what is happening. The activities may involve physical contact, including penetrative (e.g. rape or buggery) or non-penetrative acts. They may include non-contact activities, such as involving children in looking at, or in the production of, pornographic material or watching sexual activities or encouraging children to behave in sexually inappropriate ways. (The Department of Health, 1999, p. 6)

Implicit in this definition is the notion that it is harmful for children to be exposed to materials of a sexual nature. Working with children and young people therefore requires us to find a balance between disregarding important issues of sexuality on the one hand, and exposing children and young people to sexual issues that they are not yet emotionally prepared for.

An important point to note here is that sexual abuse of children arises in part from the abuse of the power of adults over children and, as such, has parallels with elder abuse which is also premised on an abuse of power.

Ageism and disablism

There are many parallels between old age and disability. Indeed, a key part of ageist ideology is the assumption that old age itself can be seen as a form of disability. Such a discriminatory attitude which denies the vitality that is often associated with older people combines with discriminatory assumptions about disabled people to produce a far from satisfactory situation.

The 'social model of disability' (Oliver and Sapey, 1999) is based on the premise that disability is caused not by physical impairments themselves, but rather by the way society treats disabled people. That is, it is the tendency to marginalise, exclude, dehumanise and patronise people with disabilities that disables them. In short, disability is socially constructed. The same logic can be applied to older people. That is, it is often ageist attitudes, assumptions and structures that cause older people problems, perhaps more so than the effects of being 'elderly' or of having a particular impairment or illness that accompanies their ageing. In this respect, older people are also to some extent disabled by society.

A consequence of equating old age with disability is that it can serve to strengthen the link in people's minds between old age, frailty and dependency. And a further consequence of that process is the assumption that ill-health or disability in old age is caused by the ageing process and therefore has a certain inevitability about it which justifies giving it little attention or priority. Furthermore, Zarb (1993) points out that many disabled people are now living beyond their sixtieth year and so experiencing both disablism and ageism. In referring to what he describes as a disability 'career' he comments on how identity and a sense of control can be hard won but become threatened again by ageist assumptions as people with disabilities grow older:

> Many older people perceive the achievement of independence (however they may define it) to be one of the most significant features of their lives throughout the disability career. Achieving this independence will often have taken many years and will certainly have involved a great deal of effort. Further, it is important to emphasise that 'independence' is not a fixed state, and maintaining control over their lives will often become increasingly hard as people grow older. Consequently, it is easy to see why the possibility of losing some of this control should be a source of great anxiety for many people . . . subjective responses to ageing are also shaped by social and material resources . . . When potential problems, such as the lack of appropriate living options, inadequate pensions and enforced dependency on ageing carers, are added to this objective reality, it is not difficult to see why many older disabled people feel that ageing represents a threat to their independence. (p. 193)

This extract does not reflect the complexities of Zarb's analysis but should serve to remind us of the interaction between ageism and other forms of discrimination. His reference to what he describes as the 'multiple jeopardies' encountered by disabled women and disabled people from ethnic minority groups, as they add age discrimination to their experiences, can only reinforce these links.

Children and young people can also experience a combination of ageism and disablism, which serves to exclude them from mainstream activities. Disabled children are often marginalised (Beresford, 2002) but, as with children and young people in general, are not always given the same chance to challenge this as are adults with more confidence and opportunity. Lansdown (2001) makes the following point about the competence of children and young people:

> The welfare model of childcare has perpetuated the view that children lack the capacity to contribute to their own well-being or do not have a valid and valuable contribution to make. Yet a failure to involve children in decisions that affect their own lives has been the cause of many of the mistakes and poor judgements exercised by adults when acting on children's behalf . . . children, even when very young, can act,

for example, as peer counsellors, mediators or mentors for other children. Local and health authorities have successfully involved children in the development of new hospitals, anti-poverty strategies and advice services. In other words far from being 'in waiting' until they acquire adult competencies, children can, when empowered to do so, act as a source of expertise, skill and information for adults and contribute towards meeting their own needs. (p. 93)

Being perceived as competent can be a struggle for all children but, when ageist stereotypes about competence are reinforced by disablist attitudes about competence, it is not hard to see that the 'in waiting' period is likely to be much longer, if it ends at all.

Practice Focus 3.4

The Richards family had thought long and hard about Sandy's continuing education. He had been blind from birth and had a learning disability. The combination of the two factors meant that he needed a lot of attention and supervision. Given that the family had three other children, they felt that they were not always able to give him the stimulation, and the life experiences, that he needed in order to develop to his full potential. They had long considered that he might benefit from continuing his education at a residential school and despite knowing that they would all miss him, had decided to go ahead with the application for a place.

Over the next few months the family received numerous visits and Sandy must have been aware that something different was going on. He was offered a place as a full-time boarder and, although they knew that they would have to explain this to Sandy at some point, they decided that it would be in his best interests if they left this until as close as possible to the beginning of the new term, so as not to worry him. However, while playing with his brother one day he overheard his sister referring to 'when Sandy has gone away'. Understandably he was very worried about this statement, especially when his sister refused to say any more, frightened by her parents' instructions not to mention it to him. Fearing that he was being punished for something he had done wrong, he didn't dare ask his parents about it but continued to worry to the extent that he couldn't sleep or concentrate on anything. It was only when his teacher got so worried about his unusually quiet behaviour in school and a marked deterioration in his work that she broached the subject with Sandy's parents. She suggested to them that he was old enough, at eleven, to at least contribute to such a life-changing decision and that, even with his learning disability, ways could have been found to make the discussions about his future meaningful and his decision-making informed. When they reflected on their approach they realised that they had let their concerns about what was best for him, and for them, completely overshadow his need to be involved in something as important as this. They knew that they had a tendency to make decisions without reference to their children, but realised that they had been so used to thinking about what Sandy couldn't do because of his impairments, that they had lost sight of his developing competence, his increasing maturity, and his rights.

Conclusion

In Part One of the book the point was made that ageism as a form of discrimination and thus a source of oppression needs to be understood not only as a set of important issues in its own right, but also as a part of a wider canvas of discrimination, disadvantage and oppression. The relationship between different forms of oppression is not a simple or static one and individuals will experience oppression in different ways, and in different combinations of ways, at different points in their lives. In this part of the book we have explored what that means by identifying links between ageism and some of the other well-established forms of discrimination. In a short book such as this, the exploration has had to be quite limited. None the less, it is to be hoped that it has been sufficient to establish the importance of seeing ageism as part of a wider picture of social divisions and not as something to be considered in isolation.

Ignoring the importance of social divisions will mean failing to appreciate that, within the disadvantage experienced at either end of the age spectrum, some individuals will be particularly disadvantaged as a result of the interaction of ageism with other forms of discrimination. If we fall into the trap of seeing anti-ageism as isolated from other forms of discrimination, then that 'pecking order' whereby some people are seen as more 'worthy' than others will be reinforced rather than challenged in childhood, adolescence and old age.

Part Four: Guide to Further Learning

General texts

What follows is a selection of texts of a general nature, not specifically relevant to any particular age group:

Abercrombie, N. (2004) *Sociology*, Cambridge, Polity Press.

This offers an introduction to the key themes of sociology and the social context in which we live our lives. It has a particularly relevant chapter entitled 'Does Inequality Matter?'

Barry, M. and Hallett, C. (eds) (1998) *Social Exclusion and Social Work: Issues of Theory, Policy and Practice*, Lyme Regis, Russell House Publishing.

Citizenship, user marginalisation and poverty feature amongst the varied aspects of social exclusion covered by this collection of papers which, although written from a social work perspective, could have a wider application.

Bryson, V. (1999) *Feminist Debates: Issues of Theory and Political Practice*, Basingstoke, Macmillan – now Palgrave Macmillan.

This is quite a wide-ranging book which begins with a look at current strands of feminist theory and goes on to explore issues connected with race, class, the law, the state, the family, reproduction, pornography and masculinity.

Crimmens, D. and West, A. (eds) (2004) *Having Their Say – Young People and Participation: European Experiences*, Lyme Regis, RHP.

As the title suggests, this book offers a comparative look at the progress being made in terms of linking children's rights with decision making processes. Contributions come from a range of countries, including England, Ireland, Scotland, Wales, Germany, Italy, Norway, Slovenia and the Netherlands.

Jackson, S. and Jones, J. (eds) (1998) *Contemporary Feminist Theories*, Edinburgh, Edinburgh University Press.

This also covers a range of issues, including economic change, anthropology, black feminisms and psychoanalytical theory. It makes the point that diversity needs to be recognised within women's studies and, as such, has something to say about ageism.

Horwarth, J. and Shardlow, S.M. (eds) (2003) *Making Links Across Specialisms*, Lyme Regis, Russell House Publishing.

This has a social work focus and may not be of relevance to all readers. However, it contains a very accessible chapter on working with older people in ways consistent with an anti-ageist approach, as well as one on working in partnership with children.

Pilkington, A. (2003) *Racial Disadvantage and Ethnic Diversity in Britain*, Basingstoke, Palgrave Macmillan.

Amongst the many issues covered are migration, racism in the labour market, housing and education systems, and a discussion of the future of a multi-ethnic society. There is a focus on understanding how identities are formed and re-framed, which is relevant to ageism also.

Solomos, J. (2003) *Race and Racism in Britain*, 3rd edn, Basingstoke, Palgrave Macmillan.

This comprehensive book begins with a discussion of the sociology of race and an update of developments in the field, before focusing more specifically on issues such as race relations policies, race and policing, race and class, before concluding with a section on new directions and perspectives. As such it offers food for thought about how ageism intersects with racism.

Thompson, N. (2001) *Anti-discriminatory Practice*, 3rd edn, Basingstoke, Palgrave Macmillan.

This text is of relevance to those involved in all aspects of people work as it offers a framework for furthering our understanding of discrimination and oppression. Following a chapter on the theory base, in which the PCS framework is discussed as an aid to analysing discrimination and oppression in general, there are sections which focus on more specific areas such as sexism, disablism and racism.

Thompson, N. (2003) *Promoting Equality: Challenging Discrimination and Oppression* (2nd edn). Basingstoke, Palgrave Macmillan.

This book builds on the introduction laid down in *Anti-Discriminatory Practice*, and takes the reader into more complex debates, while retaining an accessible style. It contains a particularly useful chapter on the concept of power.

Thompson, N. (2003) *Communication and Language: A Handbook of Theory and Practice*, Basingstoke, Palgrave Macmillan.

This book offers a good introduction to the very large theory base that underpins language and communication studies. It recognises the power of language to contribute to oppression but also to challenge it, and is written from a premise that effective people work relies on effective communication. It covers a range of topics including the spoken word, the written word and the meaning and context of communication. In particular it provides guidance on listening skills as highlighted in Part Two, and also develops many of the issues that this exploration of age discrimination has raised.

Older people

The following focus more specifically on working with older people:

Arber, S. and Ginn, J. (eds) (1995) *Connecting Gender and Ageing*, Buckingham, Open University Press.

This edited collection has a sociological focus and serves as a reminder of how ageism does not operate in isolation from other forms of oppression, but interacts with them. The contributions are varied and include discussions about the caring role, support networks, elder abuse, and retirement.

Barnett, E. (2000) *Including the Person with Dementia in Designing and Delivering Care: 'I Need to Be Me!'* London, Jessica Kingsley.

This book focuses very strongly on personhood and the care that needs to be taken to ensure that practice values, rather than denies, what makes people unique. Where 'conventional' forms of communication are compromised by dementia the author offers strategies for promoting understanding, such as reading behaviour and interpreting 'memory-stories'. As such, it has a lot to say in terms of listening skills in particular and anti-ageist practice in general.

Biggs, S. (1993) *Understanding Ageing: Images, Attitudes and Professional Practice*, Buckingham, Open University Press.

This is a thought-provoking study which challenges the negativity which is often associated with working with older people. It is divided into three sections, namely theory, practice and perspectives. All three are of relevance to an understanding of ageism.

Bounds, J. and Hepburn, H. (1996) *Empowerment and Older People*, Birmingham, Pepar.

This short book is aimed at social care practitioners and discusses how to enable older users of care services to maintain a sense of control. It contains practical tips on how to address needs without compromising independence.

Chiva, A. and Stears, D. (eds) (2001) *Promoting the Health of Older People*, Buckingham, Open University Press.

In the foreword to this edited collection we are reminded that, as the amount of time that we spend as 'older people' is increasing, the extent to which we can rely on the state for support is tending to decrease. As the title suggests, the discussions presented by the various authors all promote the theme of health promotion and, as such, offer something of a challenge to the ageist assumption that old age is necessarily equated with ill-health, and that older people are less deserving of resources than their younger counterparts.

Evans, J.G., Pollard, S., Sikora, K. and Williams, R. (2003) *They've Had a Good Innings – Can the NHS Cope with an Ageing Population?* London, Civitas.

This short book cites recent research that highlights systematic discrimination against older people within the National Health Service. Its authors raise a lot of food for thought about causes and possible solutions, suggesting that it may be necessary to rethink the whole system through which healthcare is currently provided in Britain.

Johnson, S. (2004) (ed.) *Writing Old Age*, London, Centre for Policy on Ageing.

This is an edited collection of seminar papers which share a focus on the subjective meaning of ageing – people's lived experience. It includes a commentary on the oft-quoted poem 'Kate', and some interesting discussion of cultural imagery around ageing and residential care.

Means, R., Morbey, H. and Smith, R. (2002) *From Community to Market Care? – The Development of Welfare Services for Older People*, Bristol, The Policy Press.

This is a study of four local authorities and the ways in which each interpreted national policy about welfare provision for older people, in the period leading up to the changes imposed by the NHS and Community Care Act 1990. While its focus is historical, it highlights concerns which policymakers and practitioners continue to face, such as rationing of services, the interface between health and social care provision and the debates around residential care. This book is likely to be of interest to those wanting to get a general overview of community care issues as they affect older people.

Nolan, M., Davies, S. and Grant, G. (eds) (2001) *Working with Older People and Their Families: Key Issues in Policy and Practice*, Buckingham, Open University Press.

This collection is largely health-focused but does explore the interface between health and social care. It raises the profile of quality of life issues and, especially in the final chapter, advocates for an integrated policy which seeks to address discrimination.

Thompson, S. (2002) *From Where I'm Sitting: A Manual for Those Working with Older People in the Social Care Sector*, Lyme Regis, Russell House Publishing.

This is a training manual rather than a book, but promotes anti-ageist practice by asking the reader to consider how recipients of care and support services experience these provisions from their perspective. Its aim is to encourage partnership working that is based on respect for older people's views – that is to say, working *with*, rather than doing to, older people. Amongst its eleven chapters are those which focus on feelings, loss and grief, intimacy and abuse and also a chapter on communication. Each chapter contains exercises which are designed to heighten awareness of the potential for ageism to lead to disadvantage and promote practice based on anti-ageist principles.

Quinn, A., Snowling, A. and Denicolo, P. (2003) *Older People's Perspectives: Devising Information, Advice and Advocacy Services*, York, Joseph Rowntree Foundation.

This text is a report of study undertaken in Slough around information provision by services for older people in the statutory sector. It looks at how to address existing arrangements around information provision which marginalise older people.

Vincent, J. (2003) *Old Age*, London, Routledge.

This book, from Routledge's Key Ideas series, is clearly written and accessible to a wide range of readers. From a social science perspective the author looks at issues which include identity, the medicalisation of old age, the effects of global crises on the experience of old age, and a particularly interesting and useful discussion of intergenerationality.

Children and young people

The following may be of interest to those working with children and young people:

Butler, I. and Williamson, H. (1994) *Children Speak: Children, Trauma and Social Work*, Harlow, Longman.

This work highlights how children experience and define risk and harm and details the support that they feel they need. Although it has a child protection focus, much of it will be relevant to a wide range of work with children and young people, particularly the dynamics between children talking and adults listening.

Crimmens, D. and Pitts, J. (eds) (2000) *Positive Residential Practice: Learning the Lessons of the 1990s*, Lyme Regis, Russell House Publishing.

This collection has a broad range but is structured around four themes, one of which is entitled 'The Voice of the Child'. This section contains excerpts from an interview with care leavers, a commentary on complaints procedures and a call to accord children and young people more respect and status in general, not just in the residential system.

Dwivedi, K.N. and Varma, V.P. (eds) (1996) *Meeting the Needs of Ethnic Minority Children: A Handbook for Professionals*, London, Jessica Kingsley.

This collection raises issues about a wide range of situations where the needs of children from ethnic minority groups need to be considered and debated. Amongst those included are the fields of education, health and community work.

Foley, P., Roche, J. and Tucker, S. (eds) (2001) *Children in Society: Contemporary Theory, Policy and Practice*, Basingstoke, Palgrave Macmillan.

As its title suggests, this collection integrates theory with practice and covers debates around social policy and service provision across a range of disciplines, including healthcare, social work and education. Promoting the right of children and young people to be heard is a concept which runs through many of its twenty-seven contributions.

Fraser, S., Lewis, V., Ding, S., Kellett, M. and Robinson, C. (eds) (2004) *Doing Research with Children and Young People*, London, Sage/The Open University.

A key theme of this collection of papers is the promotion of a participatory role for children and young people, so that the research is *with* them, rather than *on* them and, as such, many of the eighteen chapters challenge the perception of children as dependent, with little expertise to offer. I would suggest that the issues debated have a wider relevance than just research activity, especially that which looks at images of childhood and how its nature is socially constructed.

Hart, S., Price Cohen, C., Erickson, M.F. and Flekkoy, M. (2001) *Children's Rights in Education*, London, Jessica Kingsley.

This draws together a range of perspectives from a number of different countries, all themed around its title and a concern that children's rights in this field need to be urgently addressed.

McNeish, D., Newman, T. and Roberts, H. (eds) (2002) *What Works for Children? Effective Services for Children and Families*, Buckingham, Open University Press.

Amongst the research reviews covered in this edited collection are some around the issues of social exclusion and the involvement of children and young people in decision-making processes.

Ruegger, M. (ed.) (2001) *Hearing the Voice of the Child: The Representation of Children's Interests in Public Law Proceedings*, Lyme Regis, Russell House Publishing.

There are several relevant contributions within this collection, including the child's perspective on decision-making and the Guardian ad Litem system, techniques for helping to ensure that children are heard in court proceedings, and a paper on human rights and family law.

Sutherland, H., Sefton, T. and Piachaud, D. (2003) *Poverty in Britain: The Impact of Government Policy since 1997*, York Publishing Services.

This report raises issues about the definition of poverty and the implications of benefits and taxation changes for populations. It refers particularly to child poverty and the government's part in addressing it.

Websites

N.B. These website addresses are correct at the time of going to press but may change over time.

Older people

www.ageconcern.org.uk

This wide-ranging site has up to date news and discussions about a number of different topics which might be of interest to older people and those who support them, including information on policy changes, government initiatives on health and social care issues, welfare benefits and so on. It details the range of factsheets that are on offer to keep older people informed, such as advice on nursing and residential homes and information on local authority charging policies.

www.bgop.org.uk

This is the site of The Better Government for Older People Initiative. It covers a range of topics, including race and age diversity, lifelong learning, promoting independence and community regeneration.

www.agepositive.gov.uk

This relates to older people and employment prospects. It details the government's plans for, and commitment to, the implementation of legislation that will outlaw age discrimination in employment.

www.seniorsworld.co.uk/pensionersvoice

Here we find outlined the ethos and activities of the organisation 'Pensioners' Voice', a pressure group which lobbies the government on pensions in particular, and quality of life issues in general.

www.niace.org.uk/research/older-bolder

Compiled by the National Organisation for Adult Learning, this site details its 'older and bolder' initiative. It aims to fight marginalisation and the stereotyping of older people as 'past it' by facilitating learning opportunities for those who lack either the confidence or the means to get involved, or a combination of the two.

www.u3a.org.uk

A website highlighting The University of The Third Age's commitment to lifelong learning. It offers opportunities for older people to begin or continue studying. There is advice on setting up or joining study groups plus lists of relevant study material and it also offers online courses.

http://freespace.virgin.net/man.web.aea/

This is the site for Action on Elder Abuse and provides a number of facilities to help understand and address this important topic. It points the user to relevant literature and highlights how prevalent elder abuse is when one considers it in all its forms. In addition to incorporating a helpline the site also suggests useful links for those seeking more information.

www.seniorsnetwork.co.uk

An information resource for older people and their organisations. It houses a discussion forum, details the location of pensioners' groups around Britain, and provides updates on campaigns that are being waged at various levels.

Children and young people

www.ncb.org.uk

This is The National Children's Bureau's site. It describes its core work, which includes promoting participation and citizenship, and valuing diversity and difference. It offers an opportunity for discussion and highlights ongoing projects such as the education of children of asylum seekers and the well-being of young people in supported housing.

www.nyas.org.uk

This explains the role and activities of the National Youth Advocacy Service, which offers independent socio-legal advice to children and young people, to professionals who work in this field, and to carers and parents. It aims to establish a dialogue between its young members and policymakers.

www.childreninwales.org.uk

This bilingual site is underpinned by a commitment to making the articles of the United Nations Convention on the Rights of the Child a reality for children and young people in Wales, especially those who have special needs. An interactive section on rights is promised by the website organisers.

www.savethechildrenscot.org.uk

Amongst this site's good points are a selection of educational resources, rights-based training and a consultation toolkit.

www.childrensrights.ie/

Here the Children's Rights Alliance flags up to children and young people in Northern Ireland their rights under the United Nations Convention. It invites discussion, offers useful links and has details of relevant publications.

www.childrensrightsdirector.org.uk

This focuses on the rights of children and young people in England and has a list of links to children's rights officers and advocates.

www.nya.org.uk

The National Youth Agency works to support those working in the field of youth work to help all children and young people to fulfil their potential and participate in society. This website highlights ongoing projects and strategies, points people to a range of articles on such topics as equality and citizenship and advertises NYA publications.

www.unicef.org/crc

This site allows access to the full text of the Convention of the Rights of the Child and offers relevant statistical data. It points browsers to useful publications on the subject of rights.

Discrimination issues in general

www.eoc.org.uk

This outlines the strategies employed by the Equal Opportunities Commission in its efforts to eliminate sex discrimination. In addition to its publications list, it also has sections on relevant legislation and policy, and highlights campaigns and research in this field.

www.drc-gb.org

The Disability Rights Commission was established to promote equality of opportunity for disabled people. There is a transcript of the Disability Discrimination Act here and the site links to a helpline.

Conclusion

By its very nature age discrimination operates largely unseen and relatively unhindered. Its pervasiveness and invisibility point to just how successful and dominant an ideology it has become. As we have seen, basic citizenship rights of respect, choice and voice are often denied both older and young people. While this may sometimes be a deliberate strategy, it is as likely to arise from a lack of awareness and understanding of the discriminatory processes that can contribute towards oppression. The main aim of this book, therefore, has been to set the process of awareness raising in motion so that you will be better able to recognise discriminatory processes and strategies in the world around you, in the work you do and in the comments and actions of others. As the old adage suggests 'knowledge is power', and so it is to be hoped that, once you have become adept at recognising age discrimination, you will feel inspired to challenge it in whatever way you can.

In the present political climate, the profile of age discrimination has been given a boost by the proposed outlawing of age discrimination in the workplace, and by strategies such as the National Framework for Older People which, with its focus on providing reliable and responsive health and social care services, has offered both guidance and instruction. However, if the anti-ageist challenge is to be effective, it needs to be based on an understanding of age discrimination and its consequences, rather than on knee-jerk reactions to legal and policy directives. Ageism is too big a concept to cover in all of its complexity within the remit of this book. As I mentioned at the beginning, my aims in terms of understanding ageism have been to:

- highlight its existence;
- introduce key concepts and issues;
- provide food for thought about its consequences in terms of oppression and disadvantage; and
- get you thinking about how it can be challenged.

In his closing remarks at the United Nations conference launching the International Year of Older Persons, Kofi Annan made the following comment:

> A society for all ages is one that does not caricature older persons as patients and pensioners. Instead it sees them as both agents and beneficiaries of development . . . A Society of all ages is multi-generational . . . it is age-inclusive, with different generations recognizing – and acting upon – their commonality of interest. (1999)

Intergenerational initiatives have a common focus in their quest to use the respective skills and knowledge of people at both ends of the age spectrum to each other's mutual advantage. Referring to an intergenerational learning programme in the north of England, Stanton and Tench (2003) summarise its benefits as follows:

> In the context of the changing nature and demography of Britain's society, intergenerational activities provide a wonderful opportunity to alter the perceptions that older people have of themselves (and communities have of them) . . . (p. 76)

They go on to add:

> As with the benefits to the older volunteers, Intergenerational Learning also gives the younger generations an opportunity to become ambassadors for their age group and so help dispel the myths, stereotypes and misconceptions, which the older people may have of the young. (*ibid.*)

These comments on intergenerationality echo the message of this book, that is the need to see people of all ages as *people* and not merely as age classifications. The modern world is so complex that we need to think in terms of groups and the typifications referred to earlier if social policy, administration and practice is to be possible. But we need to remember that, while classification by age might have benefits in some respects, it should never be a justification for treating, or allowing individuals to be treated, in ways that are demeaning, disadvantaging or disempowering. We have seen that ageism operates at a number of different levels and have considered that ageism is inherent in the structures that provide the frameworks by which we live. As Higgs (1997) comments of structured dependency:

> it is ageism not biology that dominates the lives of most older people. The problems that older people face in Britain are consequently ones that can be overcome by determined policy and through realizing the full possibilities of citizenship. (p. 121)

Therein lies the anti-ageist challenge: to work towards dispelling ageist myths, undermining ageist stereotypes and ensuring that no one is denied their citizenship rights on the grounds of age. It will not be an easy task, but I hope this introduction will have inspired you to read further and play whatever part you can.

References

Arber, S. and Ginn, J. (eds) (1995) *Connecting Gender and Ageing: A Sociological Approach*, Buckingham, Open University Press.

Aries, P. (1962) *Centuries of Childhood: A Social History of Family Life*, New York, Vintage.

Baldwin, N. (2000) 'Protecting Children: Promoting Their Rights', in Baldwin (2000).

Baldwin, N. (ed.) (2000) *Protecting Children: Promoting Their Rights*, London, Whiting and Birch.

Baldwin, S. and Hirst, M. (2002) 'Children as Carers', in Bradshaw (2002).

Barnett, E. (2000) *Including the Person With Dementia in Designing and Delivering Care: I Need to be Me!*, London, Jessica Kingsley.

Bennett, G., Kingston, P. and Penhale, B. (1997) *The Dimensions of Elder Abuse: Perspectives for Practitioners*, Basingstoke, Palgrave Macmillan.

Beresford, B. (2002) 'Preventing the Social Exclusion of Disabled Children', in McNeish *et al.* (2002).

Beresford, P. and Croft, S. (1993) *Citizen Involvement: A Practical Guide for Change*. London, Palgrave Macmillan.

Bernard, M. and Meade, K. (eds) (1993) *Women Come of Age*, London, Edward Arnold.

Bevan, D. and Thompson, N. (2003) 'The Social Basis of Loss and Grief: Age, Disability and Sexuality', *Journal of Social Work* 3(2) pp. 179-194.

Blakemore, K. and Boneham, M. (1994) *Age, Race and Ethnicity: a Comparative Approach*, Buckingham, Open University Press.

Bond, J., Coleman, P. and Peace, S. (1993) *Ageing in Society: An Introduction to Social Gerontology*, 2nd edn, London, Sage.

Bradshaw, E. (ed.) (2002) *The Well-being of Children in the UK, London*, Save the Children/The University of York.

Brown, H. (2002) 'Vulnerability and Protection', Unit 18 of Course K202 *Care, Welfare and Community*, Milton Keynes, The Open University.

Bulmer, M. and Solomos, J. (eds) (1999) *Racism*, Oxford, Oxford University Press.

Burr, V. (1995) *An Introduction to Social Constructionism*, London, Routledge.

Cameron, D. (ed.) (1998) *The Feminist Critique of Language: A Reader*, 2nd edn, London, Routledge.

Channer, Y. and Parton, N. (1990) 'Racism, Cultural Relativism and Child Protection', in The Violence Against Children Study Group (1990).

Chiva, A. and Stears, D. (eds) (2001) *Promoting the Health of Older People: The Next Step in Health Generation*, Buckingham, Open University Press.

Clegg, A. (2003) 'Out of the Frame'. *Guardian Society*, September 3rd.

Coles, B. and Maile, S. (2002) 'Children, Young People and Crime', in Bradshaw (2002).

Connell, R.W. (2002) *Gender*, Cambridge, Polity Press.

Corby, B. (1989) 'Alternative Theory Bases in Child Abuse', in Stainton Rogers *et al.* (1989).

Cranny-Francis, A., Waring, W., Stavropoulos, P. and Kirby, J. (2003) *Gender Studies: Terms and Debates*, Basingstoke, Palgrave Macmillan.

Culley, L. and Dyson, S. (eds) (2001) *Ethnicity and Nursing Practice*, Basingstoke, Palgrave Macmillan.

Cummings, E and Henry, W. E. (1961) *Growing Old*, New York, Basic Books.

Davies, M. (ed.) (2000) *The Blackwell Encyclopaedia of Social Work*, Oxford, Blackwell.

Davies, M. (2001) 'Health Promotion and Sexuality in Later Life', in Chiva and Stears (2001).

Department of Health (1999) *Working Together: A Guide to Interagency Working to Safeguard and Promote the Welfare of Children*, London, HMSO.

Department of Health (2001) *National Service Framework for Older People*, London, HMSO.

Doka, K.J. (ed.) (1989) *Disenfranchised Grief: Recognising Hidden Sorrow*, Lexington, MA Lexington.

Doka, K.J. (ed.) (1995) *Children Mourning: Mourning Children*, Washington, Hospice Foundation of America.

Dwivedi, K.N. and Varma, V.P. (eds) (1996) *Meeting the Needs of Ethnic Minority Children: A Handbook for Professionals*, London, Jessica Kingsley Publishers.

Dyson, S. and Smaje, C. (2001) 'The Health Status of Minority Ethnic Groups', in Culley and Dyson (2001).

Eastman, M. (ed.) (1994) *Old Age Abuse: a New Perspective*, 2nd edn, London, Chapman and Hall.

Evans, J.G., Pollard, S., Sikora, K. and Williams, R. (2003) *They've Had a Good Innings Can the NHS Cope With an Ageing Population?* London, Civitas.

Fennell, G., Phillipson, C. and Evers, H. (1988) *The Sociology of Old Age*, Milton Keynes, Open University Press.

Foley, P., Roche, J. and Tucker, S. (eds) (2001) *Children in Society: Contemporary Theory, Policy and Practice*, Basingstoke, Palgrave Macmillan.

Freire. P. (1972) *Pedagogy of the Opressed*, Harmondsworth, Penguin.

Friedan, B. (1993) *The Fountain of Age*, London, Jonathan Cape.

German, G. (1996) 'Anti-Racist Strategies for Educational Performance: Facilitating Successful Learning for All Children', in Dwivedi and Varma (1996).

Gibson, H.B. (1992) *The Emotional and Sexual Lives of Older People*, London, Chapman and Hall.

Giddens, A. (ed.) (1997) *Sociology: Introductory Readings*, 2nd edn, Cambridge, Polity Press.

Gilligan, R. (2001) *Promoting Resilience: A Resource Book on Working with Children in the Care System*, London, BAAF.

Ginn, J. and Arber, S. (1995) 'Only Connect: Gender Relations and Ageing' in Arber and Ginn (1996).

Grant, G. (2001) 'Older People with Learning Disabilities: Health, Community Inclusion and Family Caregiving', in Nolan *et al.* (2001).

Harrison, R., Mann, G., Murphy, M., Taylor, A. and Thompson, N. (2003) *Partnership Made Painless: A Joined Up Guide to Working Together*, Lyme Regis, Russell House Publishing.

Henwood, M. and Harding, T. (2002) 'Age-Old Problem', *Community Care*, 7th March.

Hickey, G. (1994) 'Towards a Responsive Service', *Community Care*, 26th May.

Higginbottom, K. (2002) 'The Wonder Years', *People Management*, 5 December, pp 14–15.

Higgs, P. (1997) 'Citizenship Theory and Old Age: From Citizenship Rights to Surveillance', in Jamieson *et al.* (1997).

Hillyard, P., Kelly, G., McLaughlin, E., Patsios, D. and Tomlinson, M. (2003) *Bare Necessities: Poverty and Social Exclusion in Northern Ireland*, Belfast, Democratic Dialogue.

Hockey, J. and James, A. (1993) *Growing Up and Growing Old: Ageing and Dependency in the Life Course*, London, Sage.

Hopkins, G. (2002a) *Plain English for Social Services: A Guide to Better Communication*, Lyme Regis, Russell House Publishing.

Hopkins, G. (2002b) *The Write Stuff: A Guide to Effective Writing in Social Care and Related Services*, Lyme Regis, Russell House Publishing.

Hughes, B. and Mtezuka, M. (1992) 'Social Work and Older Women: Where Have Older Women Gone?', in Langan and Day (1992).

Hughes, M. (2003) 'Are You Funky, or Just Plain Old Reliable?', *The Guardian*, 28 June.

Inman, K. (2003) 'Learning To Listen', *Guardian Society*, 26th November.

Jamieson, A., Harper, S. and Victor, C. (eds) (1997) *Critical Approaches to Ageing in Later Life*, Buckingham, Open University Press.

Johnson, M. L. (1976) 'That Was Your Life: A Biographical Approach to Later Life', in Munnichs and Van Den Heuval (1976).

Kroll, B. (2002) 'Children and Divorce', in Thompson (2002b).

Langan, M. and Day, L. (eds) (1992) *Women, Oppression and Social Work*, London, Routledge.

Lansdown, G. (2001) 'Children's Welfare and Children's Rights', in Foley *et al.* (2001).

Ledwith, S. and Colgan, F. (eds) (1996) *Women in Organisations: Challenging Gender Politics*, Basingstoke, Macmillan.

Levenson, R. (2003) *Auditing age Discrimination: A Practical Approach to Promoting Age Equality in Health and Social Care*, London, King's Fund.

Lowe, S. (2003) 'In Need of an Anchor', *Community Care* 2–8 October.

Lustbader, W. (1991) *Counting on Kindness: The Dilemmas of Dependency*, New York, The Free Press.

Marlow, A. and Loveday, B. (eds) (2000) *After Macpherson: Policing after the Stephen Lawrence Inquiry*, Lyme Regis, Russell House Publishing.

Masters, S. (2003) 'Earning Young People's Respect', *Professional Social Work*, January.

McCullagh, C. (2002) *Media Power: A Sociological Introduction*, Basingstoke, Palgrave Macmillan.

McKay, M., Davies, M. and Fanning, P. (1995) *Messages: The Communication Skills Handbook*, 2nd edn, Oakland, New Harbinger Publications.

McNeish, D., Newman, T. and Roberts, H. (eds) (2002) *What Works for Children?* Buckingham, Open University Press.

Midwinter, E. (1990) An Ageing World: The Equivocal Response, *Ageing And Society 10*.

Morgan, J. D. (ed.) (1996) *Ethical Issues in the Care of the Dying and Bereaved Aged*, New York, Baywood Publishing Company.

Moss, M. S. and Moss, S. Z. (1989) 'Death of the Very Old', in Doka (1989).

Munnichs, J. M. A., and Van Den Heuval, W. J. A. (eds) (1976) *Dependency or Interdependency in Old Age*, The Hague, Martinus Nijhoff.

Nolan, M., Davies, S. and Grant, G. (eds) (2001) *Working With Older People and Their Families: Key Issues in Policy and Practice*, Buckingham, Open University Press.

Norman, A. (1985) *Triple Jeopardy*, London, Centre for Policy on Ageing.

Office for National Statistics (2001) *General Household Survey*, London, ONS.

Oliver, M. and Sapey, B. (1999) *Social Work with Disabled People*, 2nd edn, Basingstoke, Palgrave Macmillan.

O'Rourke, L. (2002) *For the Record: Recording Skills Training Manual*, Lyme Regis, Russell House Publishing.

Owusu-Bempah, K. (2001) 'Racism: An Important Factor in Practice with Ethnic Minority Children and Families', in Foley *et al.* (2001).

Phillipson, C. (1982) *Capitalism and the Construction of Old Age*, Basingstoke, Macmillan.

Pilkington, A. (2003) *Racial Disadvantage and Ethnic Diversity in Britain*, Basingstoke, Palgrave.

Pritchard, J. (1994) 'Social Work Practice in Dealing With Abuse', in Eastman (1994).

Quilgars, D. (2002) 'The Mental Health of Children', in Bradshaw (2002).

Romaine, M. (2002) 'Adoption and Foster Care', in Thompson (2002).

Rose, H. and Bruce. E. (1995) 'Mutual Care but Differential Esteem: Caring Between Older Couples', in Arber and Ginn (1995).

Schön, D. A. (1983) *The Reflective Practitioner*, London, Temple Smith.

Searle, B. (2002) 'Youth Suicide', in Bradshaw (2002).

Solomos, J. (2003) *Race and Racism in Britain*, 2nd edn, Basingstoke, Palgrave Macmillan.

Spiers, H. (2003) 'If it's good enough for . . .' *Young People Now*, 12–18th March.

Stainton Rogers, W., Hevey, D. and Ash, E. (eds) (1989) *Child Abuse and Neglect: Facing the Challenge*, London, Batsford.

Stanton, G. and Tench, P. (2003) 'Intergenerational Storyline: Bringing the Generations Together in North Tyneside', *Journal of Intergenerational Relationships* , 1(1).

Storkey, E. (1991) 'Race, Ethnicity and Gender', Open University, Unit 8 of D103, *Society and Social Science*.

Strong, S. (2003) 'Different Voices, Single Harmony', *Care and Health* Issue 37 (June 4th – 17th).

Swain, J., Finkelstein, V., French, S. and Oliver, M. (1993) *Disabling Barriers – Enabling Environments*, London, Sage.

Thomas, N. (2001) 'Listening to Children', in Foley *et al.* (2001).

Thompson, N. (1992) 'Age and Citizenship', *Elders: The Journal of Care and Practice* 1(1) (downloadable from www.neilthompson.info).

Thompson, N. (1995) *Age and Dignity: Working with Older People*, Aldershot, Arena.

Thompson, N. (1996) 'Tackling Ageism – Moral Imperative or Current Fad?', in Morgan (1996).

Thompson, N. (2000) *Theory and Practice in Human Services*, 2nd edn, Buckingham, Open University Press.

Thompson, N. (2001) *Anti-Discriminatory Practice*, 3rd edn, Basingstoke, Palgrave Macmillan.

Thompson, N. (2002a) *Building the Future: Social Work with Children, Young People and Their Families*, Lyme Regis, Russell House Publishing.

Thompson, N, (ed.) (2002b) *Loss and Grief: A Guide for Human Services Practitioners*, Basingstoke, Palgrave Macmillan.

Thompson, N. (2003) *Communication and Language: A Handbook of Theory and Practice*, Basingstoke, Palgrave Macmillan.

Thompson, N. and Thompson, S. (2002) *Understanding Social Care*, Lyme Regis, Russell House Publishing.

Thompson, S. (1997) *User Involvement: Giving Older People a Voice*, Wrexham, Prospects Publications.

Thompson, S. (2002) 'Older People', in Thompson (2002b).

Thornton, P. and Tozer, R. (1995) *Having a Say in Change: Older People and Community Care*, York, Joseph Rowntree Foundation.

UNICEF (2003) *Child Poverty in the Developing World*, downloadable from www.uni-cef.org/media/files/Childpoverty.pdf.

Vincent, J. (2003) *Old Age*, London, Routledge.

Vincent, C., Riddell, J. and Shmueli, A. (2000) *Sexuality and the Older Woman – An Executive Summary*, Huddersfield, Pennell Initiative for Women's Health.

Violence Against Children Study Group (1990) *Taking Child Abuse Seriously*, London, Unwin Hyman.

Walker, A. (1993) 'Poverty and Inequality in Old Age', in Bond *et al.* (1993).

Wise, S. (2000) 'Heterosexism', in Davies (2000).

Woolf, J. and Woolf, M. (2003) *Caring For an Older Person with Failing Memory*, Wirral, Gorselands.

Zarb, G. (1993) 'The Dual Experience of Ageing with a Disability', in Swain *et al.* (1993).

Index